NO CONDITION PERMANENT

For
My Son Rowan
Who Wisely Persuaded Me to Obtain
an Appropriate Technology for Writing this Book

No Condition Permanent

Pump-priming Ghana's Industrial Revolution

IAN SMILLIE

INTERMEDIATE TECHNOLOGY PUBLICATIONS
1986

Intermediate Technology Publications
9 King Street, London WC2E 8HW, UK

© IT Publications, 1986

ISBN 0 946688 32 X

Typeset in Great Britain by
Photobooks (Bristol) Ltd.
and printed by WBC Print Ltd, Bristol

Contents

Currency Equivalents

All cedi equivalents used in this book have been converted at the rate of exchange prevailing during the period described.

	US$	Cedis
February 1973—June 1978	1	= 1.15
After June 1978	1	= 2.75
After April 1983	1	=24.69
After October 1983	1	=35.00
After March 1984	1	=38.50
After December 1984	1	=50.00
After April 1985	1	=53.00
After January 1986	1	=90.00

Important Dates

5 March 1957	British Crown Colony, The Gold Coast, becomes the first black colony in Africa to achieve independence; under the Prime Ministership (later Presidency) of Kwame Nkrumah, name is changed to Ghana; Republican constitution introduced, July 1960.
25 February 1966	Military coup establishes the National Liberation Council under the Leadership of General Ankrah; March 1969, Ankrah resigns and is replaced by Brigadier Akwasi Afrifah.
October 1969	Return to civilian rule; Second Republic established under Prime Ministership of Kofi Busia.
13 January 1972	Second Military Coup; National

Redemption Council established under Chairmanship of Colonel Ignatius Acheampong.

15 July 1978   Third Coup; Acheampong replaced by Lieutenant-General Fred Akuffo.

4 June 1979   Fourth Coup; Akuffo regime replaced by Armed Forces Revolutionary Council under the Chairmanship of Flight-Lieutenant Jerry Rawlings.

24 September 1979   Return to civilian rule; AFRC hands over to newly elected President Hilla Limann.

31 December 1981   Fifth coup overthrows Third Republic; civilians replaced by the Provisional National Defence Council under Chairmanship of Flight-Lieutenant Jerry Rawlings.

Acronyms

AT	Appropriate Technology
ATDA	Appropriate Technology Development Association (India)
CEMAT	Centro de Estudios Mesoamericanos y de Technologia Apropida (Guatemala)
CIDA	Canadian International Development Agency
DAPIT	Development and Application of Intermediate Technology
EEC	European Economic Community
GCE	General Certificate of Education
GDP	Gross Domestic Product
GOG	Government of Ghana
IDRC	International Development Research Centre (Canada)
IITA	International Institute for Tropical Agriculture (Nigeria)
ITDG	Intermediate Technology Development Group (UK)
ITTU	Intermediate Technology Transfer Unit
NCWD	National Council on Women and Development (Ghana)
NIEO	New International Economic Order
NGO	Non-governmental Organization
ODA	Overseas Development Administration (UK)
OECD	Organization for Economic Co-operation and Development
PNDC	Provisional National Defence Council (Ghana)

TCC	Technology Consultancy Centre (Ghana)
UNDP	United Nations Development Programme
UNESCO	United Nations Educational, Scientific and Cultural Organization
UNICEF	United Nations Children's Fund
USAID	United States Agency for International Development
UST	University of Science and Technology (Ghana)
VSO	Voluntary Service Overseas (UK)

Acknowledgements

On my last day in Ghana, in May 1985, I stood by the sea front at the old harbour in the Jameston section of Accra and watched as the turquoise waves, rolling in from the Gulf of Guinea, crashed against the breakwater. The harbour, once the point from which surf-boats set off to lighter goods ashore from steamers plying the West African coast, is now the centre of a different form of industry—a small Ghanaian company has leased the site as a workshop for boatmaking; small wooden diesel-powered fishing boats, and larger ones up to 22 metres in length. That day, 250 men, 60 of them carpenters, were at work constructing 15 different boats, some for local fishermen, some for customers as far away as Sierra Leone. The purpose of my visit was to see how nuts and bolts made in Kumasi were being used to sustain an important Accra enterprise. Looking west along the coast, through the mist rising from the breakers, at the far end of the city I could see the huge elliptical arches in Black Star Square where Kwame Nkrumah had proclaimed the independence of Ghana 28 years before, the point to which I had gravitated on the first day of my first visit to Ghana in 1967.

Since then, I have travelled to Ghana many times, but few visits were as enjoyable as the one during which this book was researched. The pleasure was a reflection of the fact that for the first time in many years, economic conditions in Ghana seemed to be on an upswing. But it was also enjoyable because of the traditional warmth and friendliness of Ghanaian people, and because of the considerable assistance I received in gathering information and impressions. I am grateful to the many representatives of government and international agencies in Accra, Kumasi and Tamale who gave me their time and assistance. The advice and background information provided by professors and lecturers at the University of Science and Technology was much appreciated, as was the time given by many individuals in towns and villages visited in the course of my work. I owe a special vote of thanks to past and absent TCC staff whose writings and records are lasting testimony to their achievements. And I am particularly grateful to Dr John Powell who took much time from his demanding work to be with me or to make sure I got to where I was going, and to explain many things to me, often more than once.

Among the many who gave generously of their time, I would like to thank Nana Edward Abrefah, Peter Adade, Kwame Appiah, Samuel Arthur, Edward Asante-Frempong, Frank Awuah, Solomon and Ben Adjorlolo, Archibald Boateng, Archie Book, Daniel Cheku, Willie Clarke-Okah, Julie Dahlen, Peter Donkor, Matthew Feddon, Alhaji Issa Goodman, Joseph Kwaako, Ralph and Marlene Moshage, Francis Oduro-Boateng, S.A. Okunor, Peggy Oti-Boateng, Anthony Owusu-Amankwatia, Richard Wilkinson, Gilbert Workey, Chris D'Souza, and especially Frank Robertson. I am grateful to Mr R.C. Dellow of Meggit Machine Tools and Equipment, Dorset —TCC's long-time supplier of reconditioned equipment—for information on the historical prices of machine tools. I should add that opinions contained in this book are mine alone, and do not necessarily reflect the view of any other individual or organization.

I am also grateful to ITDG for giving me the opportunity to experience an industrial revolution at first hand, and to see those waves rolling off the Gulf of Guinea once again.

Ian Smillie
London
January 1986

Photographs provided by John Powell and Ian Smillie.

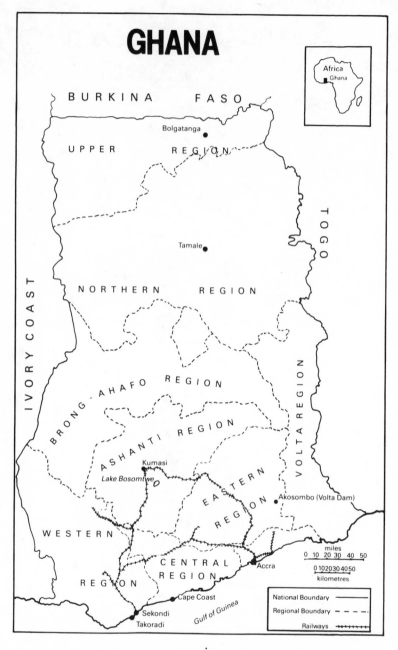

GHANA

Africa
Ghana

BURKINA   FASO

Bolgatanga ●

UPPER   REGION

TOGO

Tamale ●

NORTHERN   REGION

BRONG-AHAFO   REGION

IVORY COAST

ASHANTI   REGION

Kumasi ●
Lake Bosomtwe

VOLTA REGION

EASTERN

REGION

● Akosombo (Volta Dam)

WESTERN

CENTRAL
REGION

REGION

● Accra

Cape Coast ●

Sekondi
Takoradi

Gulf of Guinea

miles
0 10 20 30 40 50

0 1020304050
kilometres

National Boundary ————
Regional Boundary – – –
Railways ┼┼┼┼┼

xvi

CHAPTER 1
Roughness, Pimples and Warts

Mr Lely, I desire you would use all your skill to paint my picture truly like me, and not flatter me at all; but remark all these roughnesses, pimples, warts and everything as you see me, otherwise I will never pay a farthing for it.

Oliver Cromwell

This book is about mistakes, and luck, and a few genuine victories that emerged, as most victories do, from long struggle. It is about the beginning of an industrial revolution that was postponed for almost three centuries. It is about the development of 'appropriate' technology; but to a greater extent, it is about the much trickier and less successful business of transferring technology. The book is about the hard-won lessons that emerged from a long and sometimes painful search both for appropriate hardware and for a workable technique for applying it in the cause of human development. The story takes place in Ghana, but it could perhaps have happened almost anywhere in Africa, or, for that matter, in any country that has made a tryst with the ravenous, winged harpy of industrialization and found the experience to be socially unrewarding and economically unfulfilling. It focuses on an institution in Kumasi called the Technology Consultancy Centre, one of dozens, if not hundreds of appropriate technology institutions—'AT Centres', to use the generic term—that sprang up around the world in the 1970s. This one, however, would be different.

Throughout West Africa, heavy goods vehicles, taxis, buses and passenger lorries—*tro-tros, mammy wagons, poda-podas*—are decorated with brightly coloured slogans, dire imprecations, proverbs derived from the Bible, the Koran and ancient folk-wisdom, and simple homespun mottoes created by the owner.

1

'God's Time is the Best' is a frequent reminder of human mortality as well as a cautious warning to passing drivers. 'Original Canada' on a wrecked *tro-tro*, 'One People, One Nation, One Destiny' on a disabled truck, or 'Jimmy Carter' on an abandoned, rusting taxi seem full of momentous significance and of West Africa's well-deserved reputation for wit and good humour. 'Don't Let Me Down,' 'Except God,' 'Love All, Trust Few,' and 'Ninety-nine Days for Thief, One Day for Master,' all convey different thoughts and moods which can keep travellers thinking and guessing for miles.

'No Condition Permanent', one of the most common slogans, can be found on vehicles plying roads from The Gambia to the Cameroon border, and seems to sum up the resilience, the optimism and the confidence of people and of societies where change, not always for the better, is a fact of everyday life. 'No Condition Permanent' seems a fitting title for a study of appropriate technology in Ghana, partly because for development workers in a poor society, no condition is or should be accepted as permanent. In the development and transfer of appropriate technology, this is even more true. Poverty, disease, high mortality rates, back-breaking labour, low productivity, exploitation of women, deteriorating terms of trade, are all conditions which appropriate technology seeks to affect in a positive manner. And yet, as will be seen from the experience of TCC, some of the basic canons of appropriate technology were found wanting when it came to the actual acceptance of what seemed like eminently appropriate and viable propositions. For appropriate technology, too, no condition was permanent.

There is a propensity in development writing towards a style which purports to be objective, which avoids discussion of individuals, personality clashes, corruption, the unfortunate gaffes and the unvarnished luck—good and bad—which alter and certainly illuminate our times. This tends to sanitize the issue at hand, to remove it from the context in which it exists. By ignoring the constraints under which it thrived—or failed—one is often denied both a useful learning experience and an interesting story. The value in studying TCC is not in learning about the tribulations in finding an effective formula

2

for glue made from cassava starch, or the details of a cost-effective palm oil press. There are dozens of catalogues, handbooks and journals full of formulae and plans for glue and presses and almost everything else that falls under the rubric of appropriate technology. What is interesting about the TCC experience is the route by which glue eventually became a widely produced Ghanaian product rather than an imported one. Needless to say, it did not happen as a result of professors flipping through a handbook on good ideas, stopping at gluemaking, setting up a plant and then checking it off as a success story. Greed and corruption played as large a part in the success of cassava glue as did the formula developed in university test tubes.

In another case, it took seven long years of struggle to advance from the point where TCC could produce steel nuts and bolts cheaply and simply in its own workshop, to the point where someone not connected with the university actually took up the technology. It is the account of those seven years, of the first off-campus manufacturers and what finally made the idea attractive to them, that should make the story of nuts and bolts interesting, and perhaps useful to others in the field of technology transfer. The actual technology of making nuts and bolts, while obviously of much importance to those in the workshop, is, for the purposes of this story, almost a sidelight.

The real story of TCC's first years is the story of its struggle to transfer technologies, many of which were developed in its first months. It was a struggle against entrenched societal values, against intellectual elitism and all-pervasive bureaucratic red tape, against good intentions and corruption, against logic and perversity.

The word 'corruption' has already been mentioned three times; for most books on international development, this is twice too many. Often the subject is ignored, or is subsumed under vague economic euphemisms such as 'market distortions', 'informal sector', 'shadow exchange rate', or simply 'economic inefficiencies'. This book does not dwell on corruption, but it would be impossible to write about appropriate technology in Ghana, small-scale enterprise or development in general without some reference to what Ghanaians call *kalebule*.

3

Kalebule itself is a euphemism for everything from the black market to bribery and smuggling, and in Ghana, especially through the 1970s and early 1980s, *kalebule* was a fact of everyday life for almost everyone. Its roots lay partially in Ghana's economic decline from an apparently happy, prosperous former colony, to a country racked by political, economic and ecological disaster. This, too, is an essential part of the story of TCC, for Ghana's economic decline was at least in part responsible for some of the Centre's successes. Conversely, recent government recovery programmes have cast a shadow over at least one of the TCC's major success stories, and questions have been raised about the role of government, transnational corporations, and international trade as they relate to small-scale development initiatives.

Individuals are an essential part of the TCC story, as well. There is a tendency in development literature to write about a project or a phenomenon as though it sprang from the ground, perfectly formed and without more than a policy debate or an institutional decision behind it. As somebody once said, however, you cannot have Hamlet without the Prince, and the TCC story has its share of princes, villains, and even the occasional princess. It was, for example, a combination of presumptuous expatriate hobbyists and a university political feud that combined to create the TCC, and it was the considerable continuity of key staff over 15 years that provided it with the organizational memory and the experience necessary to function effectively within the societal, economic and political constraints of Ghana's Second and Third Decades of Independence. Aid agencies play an important part in the story as well, both as mentors and as irresponsible dilettantes, whose assistance or interference alternately advanced or retarded the work of the Centre.

More than anything else, however, the story of TCC demonstrates the importance of the inter-relationships that must exist between and among institutions, policies, technologies and individuals if successful and appropriate forms of development are to occur. That tensions will exist between academics and hands-on engineers within a university is probably inevitable. That government decision-makers and aid

4

agencies must appreciate the effect of investments and policy changes on small-scale rural enterprise is essential. That increased food productivity must be matched by an equally increased capacity to process it is logical. That a direct link exists between a desirable piece of food-processing equipment and an ability to manufacture it and maintain it is only common sense. And yet the inevitable, the essential, the logical, the common sensical, all had to be learned, appreciated and absorbed into the consciousness of TCC and its work.

This is, in fact, the story of a confluence of individuals, ideas, technologies, societal values and economic conditions that came together during a particularly difficult period in the history of one of the world's most friendly countries. It is not so much about appropriate technology as it has come to be known—almost traditionally—but about how appropriate technology had to be redefined and reshaped in order to make it useful, practicable and accessible to ordinary Ghanaians in order to ensure, in the best sense of the expression, that no condition remained permanent.

CHAPTER 2
The Age of Aquarius

Astrologers and song-writers predicted that when the Moon found itself in the Seventh House, and Jupiter had aligned with Mars, the Age of Aquarius would have begun. Replacing the 2,000-year strife-torn Age of Pisces, the Aquarian age, heralded as one of unprecedented peace and harmony, is said to have dawned in 1960. Taking astrology with them to the stars, American astronauts on one of the first US moon landings unabashedly named their spacecraft 'Aquarius'. And, by chance, the hopeful Aquarian Age coincided almost exactly with the independence movement, the optimistic 'winds of change' blowing across Africa. The first, and one of the most favoured of colonial territories to break free of its British masters, was the Gold Coast, renamed Ghana after an ancient and prosperous West African Kingdom. It might be said for Ghana, however, that Independence in 1957 was something of a false start, and that by 1971, at the beginning of what the United Nations called the Second Development Decade, a new start—possibly a new age of peace and harmony—could be foreseen.

Ghana had left the colonial orbit well-endowed with both human and natural resources. Stretching north from the Accra Plains and a 334-mile coastline, forests rich in hardwoods merge with the hilly Ashanti Region, and further north the country is transformed gradually into rolling savannah which becomes more semi-arid near the border with Burkina Faso. Roughly the size of West Germany, Ghana inherited large deposits of diamonds, gold, bauxite and manganese, as well as untapped reserves of limestone, iron ore and offshore oil. There was a good supply of arable land for cereal and starchy staples, and Ghanaians enjoyed considerable benefits from fishing and forestry. Except for rice, Ghana was self-sufficient in foodcrops, and was the world's largest exporter of cocoa beans. There were 20,000 miles of road, 800 miles of railway, and a healthy balance of payments. At independence, Ghana's six or seven million people enjoyed a higher literacy rate, better health care and a standard of living that was higher than any other country in West Africa.

This idealized, even nostalgic portrait of a country born with a silver spoon in its mouth is misleading, however. Development had been badly skewed towards extractive industries and primary commodities. The railway serviced only the 'golden triangle' between Accra, Kumasi and the port of Takoradi, and north of Ashanti the country was badly neglected. The flourishing export sector, dominated by cocoa, contrasted sharply with a stagnating agricultural base. Kwame Nkrumah, Ghana's first Prime Minister and later President, a prominent Pan-Africanist and an outspoken anti-colonialist, popularized the concept of neo-colonialism, citing as illustrations Ghana's dependence upon metropolitan cocoa speculators, and the foreign ownership, profit extraction and management of almost all of Ghana's industry.

Nkrumah equated industrialization with development, believing, as many economists did at the time, that growth could become self-sustaining once it reached a critical 'take-off' point, and that what was required was a 'big push', a massive investment, especially in industrialization. Industrialization, it was felt, would form important linkages with various sectors of the economy, by supplying other industries and agriculture, or by increasing the demand for their products as inputs. Because private enterprise was neither a desirable vehicle for Nkrumah's socialist modernization, nor a practical source for the level of investment he sought, accelerated industrialization was to be achieved through massive planned state intervention in the economy.

His government embarked on a strenuous effort to transform Ghana from a primarily agrarian to a partially industrialized state, making huge investments in both productive and service-oriented State Enterprises and State Farms, improving the road network, constructing a modern port at Tema, embarking on the massive Volta Lake project which would

7

provide electricity for industry, introducing universal primary education, and vastly expanding secondary and university facilities.

By 1972, however, the hope of Ghana's First Decade of Independence lay in tatters. Alarmed or attracted—depending on their proclivities and their politics—by Nkrumah's forceful rhetoric, aid donors had either made themselves scarce or had been enticed into massive State Farms and other show-piece projects. Major economic decisions had been made for social or political reasons, often with minimal reference to concepts of efficiency or profitability. While manufacturing as a percentage of Gross Domestic Product had risen from 10 per cent in 1960, to 14 per cent in 1970, most new enterprises were highly capital intensive and were completely dependent upon imported raw materials, spare parts and technicians for their effective operation. Some State Enterprises leeched the exchequer without ever beginning production; few achieved more than 60 per cent of capacity, mocking the ambitious plans that had been set for them and draining off precious foreign exchange. A mango canning factory was installed with a capacity that exceeded the entire world trade in canned mango products. A glass factory which could produce sheet glass in addition to bottles was selected over one that produced bottles alone, because the minister responsible wanted the most complete, modern factory available. The demand for sheet glass in Ghana was minuscule, however, and that section of the factory never began production.

The cocoa and timber sectors were ignored, setting the stage for future decline, while small-scale and traditional producers were driven from their workshops by inflation and the mass-produced goods that flowed erratically from State Enterprises. Industry and agriculture alike suffered from a growing proclivity towards government control and intervention, while Westminster-style democracy was replaced by a preventive detention act and a single-party constitution. Despite criticism of the elitist educational system handed down from the colonial power, Ghana had been unable to find an effective alternative, and urban drift led to growing unemployment and dissatisfaction among increasingly literate but unskilled youth

8

seeking white-collar jobs. Spending continued despite a disastrous fall in the world price of cocoa—from £467 a ton in 1954, to £140 a ton in 1965—by which time Ghana was all but bankrupt. The sad irony was that Nkrumah, the great nationalist, had sought Ghana's salvation in imported modern technology rather than in the consolidation and improvement of traditional techniques.

The military government that seized power in a 1966 coup halted some of the more reckless spending, but maintained Nkrumah's commitment to economic nationalism without improving efficiency, production or social conditions. And so, when the military transferred power to a democratically elected civilian regime three years later, Ghana was a sadder but presumably wiser country, one in which a number of important lessons had been learned, and one that seemed ready for a second starting gun.

Reading a magazine

While the terms 'intermediate' and 'appropriate technology' had yet to gain popularity, it was understood in Ghana that much of the development effort and the technologies chosen for its propagation in the first years of independence, in both agriculture and manufacturing, had been inappropriate to the country's needs, as well as to its human and economic resource base. There was also a growing recognition among industrialized countries and aid agencies that Third World development would require more than the 'quick fix' approach of the Marshall Plan and the First Development Decade. The need for a long term, integrated approach, with much more careful attention to the choice of technology and the methodology of its transfer, was eloquently, if fleetingly expressed by former Canadian Prime Minister, Lester Pearson, in his 1970 World Bank-sponsored study, *Partners in Development*[1]. Less eloquent, but destined to become more tangible in its development impact on Ghana, was a fortuitous combination of people, events and attitudes that united at roughly the same time to form the Technology Consultancy Centre in Kumasi.

Kumasi, the 'Garden City', ancient heart of the Ashanti

people, seat of their traditional ruler, the Asantehene, and centre of the cocoa growing industry, is today a regional capital of about 350,000 people, and home of the University of Science and Technology. UST, or 'Tech' as it is sometimes called in Kumasi, was founded in 1951 as a university college and was raised to full university status in 1960. Today, 3,000 students, of whom roughly 600 are women, attend classes in a standard range of undergraduate faculties with an emphasis, as the name implies, on science and technology. Most of the faculty is Ghanaian, but in the late 1960s, a high proportion were expatriates, some of whom looked beyond the classroom and took an interest in the practical side of technology transfer.

Kumasi was an ideal place for the amateur innovator, inventor and tinkerer. As a traditional crossroads, historically and strategically located for optimum north-south and east-west trade, at the heartland of cocoa and situated at the apex of the modern-day golden triangle, Kumasi was, in many ways, a more active and vital city than the capital, Accra, 250 kilometres to the south. For here in Kumasi was the site of one of the largest traditional markets in West Africa. And here, too, was one of the biggest open-air informal industrial areas in the world, Suame Magazine. Originally located near the town centre on the site of an old military depot, the industrial area grew so large that city officials moved it to Suame on the northern edge of Kumasi, to which, along with their skills and equipment, the artisans also took the name, 'magazine'.

Today, there are an estimated 40,000 workers in Suame Magazine, covering an area of hundreds of acres rolling eastward away from the Kumasi-Offinso road, up the hills beyond, and stretching north, past the city limits, encroaching on the farms and lands of neighbouring chieftaincies. An overwhelming first impression of Suame, after dust in the dry season and mud during the rains, is noise; the roar of diesels, the hum of electric motors, shouts, and endless hammering— blacksmiths, men straightening steel rods, panel beaters, carpenters, demolition experts. Water and sanitation in Suame are in short supply, electricity is erratic, roads, where they are passable, are bound together by junk, scrap metal and even discarded engine blocks which poke through the mud. Most of the hundreds of enterprises are housed in shacks of wood and corrugated sheet, and few employ more than half a dozen workers. But amidst the noise and dirt and apparent chaos, there is an incredible sense of industry and vitality. Vehicle repair is the primary enterprise, a steady growth industry after imports of new vehicles and spares began to decline and as Ghana's roads fell into worse and worse repair. Each shop seems to have a speciality: 'Doctor of Volkswagen', says one sign; 'Mister Brakes', another.

By and large, techniques and equipment are rudimentary. Disembowelled trucks and cars litter the Magazine; engines are lifted out of vehicles and replaced by hand—many hands. But while the most amazing repairs are attempted, often successfully, they can be time-consuming and costly, and are often done without useful, and sometimes essential theoretical knowledge of materials, safety, or engineering. One study revealed that while some shops were capable of reboring an engine or grinding valves, none of the workers understood how an internal combustion engine worked, making simple diagnosis, testing and maintenance virtually impossible.

There is some production in Suame Magazine: woodwork, the occasional one-off part designed to get a lorry back on the road; crude bits and pieces hammered out of scrap steel or cut from old inner tubes; but repair was and remains the first enterprise, with trade the second. Everywhere in Suame Magazine there are traders. One shop specializes in glass or steel taken from wrecks, another in used jacks, a third in nuts and bolts, laboriously removed from derelicts. One woman presides over a cache of wire—copper, steel, aluminium—coiled on nails on the walls of her shop; another sits by a stand where dozens of small blobs of grease, portioned out on pieces of cardboard, are available for 10 cedis each.

A 1971 UST survey of Suame, then much smaller than today, found more than 1,600 separate owner-operated businesses, including 1,100 workshops, of which 500 were involved in vehicle repair or modification and 300 were speciality shops offering welding, or carpentry or blacksmithing. There were 150 dealers in vehicles and spare parts. Suame Magazine was a vibrant, exciting place, and it acted as a

In Suame Magazine everything revolved around trade or repairs.

powerful magnet for engineers from UST, some of whom joined together to establish an informal association called the Kumasi Technology Group. Although there was no coherent expression of what the engineers wanted to do, Suame seemed to represent the quintessential Ghana, a place where practical technology of the sort that mattered to real people was being used every day of the week; if a university of science and technology was to be relevant to society, somehow it had to relate to a place like Suame.

The Technology Consultancy Centre

That most of the 40 UST faculty members who joined the Kumasi Technology Group were expatriates is perhaps not surprising. It is expatriates on short and usually lucrative contracts, with few social, family or financial obligations, who have both the time and the presumption to offer solutions to seemingly intractable social and technical problems. Perhaps because of its presumption and lack of organization, the Kumasi Technology Group never quite became the focus of innovation its members had in mind, and they spent much of their time installing new machinery or repairing existing equipment far from Suame. But it was a start, and it was one of the two strands that came together eventually to form the Technology Consultancy Centre. The second, and probably more fundamental strand, was a political dispute that had simmered on the campus for some time. It was the practice of the country's three universities to pay a salary supplement to doctors in medical faculties, in order to compensate them for the loss of income they might otherwise expect to receive through private practice and consultancies. At UST, many of the professors in science, engineering and architecture felt that they should either be similarly compensated, or allowed to undertake private consultancies.

In an effort to defuse this problem, the university invited the London-based Intermediate Technology Development Group to assist in developing a solution. In 1970, Sir John Palmer and George McRobie visited UST, and their report formed a basis for the establishment of an intermediate technology institute. Crisis became the midwife of the TCC, however, because before the Palmer-McRobie Report could be considered by the University Council, 13 engineers resigned from the faculty of engineering over the question of a professional salary supplement. The hurried recruitment of new faculty in Britain was followed by the establishment of the TCC, with one of the newly recruited professors, Dr John Powell, appointed as the first Director.

Powell was barely more than 30 at the time. While completing his undergraduate studies at the University of Southampton, he had apprenticed four years with Bristol Siddeley Engines, and after receiving a Ph.D. in mechanical engineering, spent seven years in British industry. There he concentrated on the field of air lubricated bearings, publishing a book on the subject—*The Design of Aerostatic Bearings*—in 1970. Although his work had taken him occasionally to the

13

Middle East, he had been in Ghana less than a year when he was given the job of establishing the TCC. It was an ominous task: not only was he charged with the creation of an institute of appropriate technology, without staff and without a budget, he had to reconcile the problem of professors demanding consultancies with the desire by others to 'do something useful'. At first, the two ideas seemed compatible. The TCC, formally established in January 1972, was set up as an autonomous unit within the university, reporting to the Vice Chancellor, and through the Vice Chancellor to the University Council. Unlike other faculties, it did not report to the Academic Board, but was governed by a Management Committee of the deans of all the faculties, chaired by the Vice Chancellor. In this way, each faculty had input into the Centre, but none could actually direct it, or subordinate its goals and budget to narrower faculty considerations.

It was the work of another unofficial group of professors with whom Powell had been associated, the Suame Product Development Group, which perhaps inadvertently gave TCC

Coach bolts for wooden truck bodies in Suame Magazine were one of TCC's first efforts.

14

its first sense of direction. Rooting around in Suame, they had made contact with carpenters building wooden bodies on to truck chassis, and discovered that there was a critical shortage of coach bolts. A few were being made to special order by blacksmiths in the Magazine, but they were crude and expensive. So, with little relief in sight from imports, the Suame Product Development Group began to work on an alternative. They discovered that there were half a dozen centre lathes in the Magazine, and they felt that if a reasonably good, low-cost coach bolt could be developed in the university workshops, it would be readily adopted and produced in the Magazine. A small production unit was set up in the Faculty of Engineering, two apprentices were loaned by an interested Suame artisan, and using a capstan lathe, a milling machine and a blacksmith's forge, the first batch of 192 bolts and nuts was produced—and sold—in August 1972. By the end of the year, however, only 562 nuts and bolts had been produced; meaningful production runs were constrained by other demands on the university's equipment and by the teaching requirements of the professors.

It had become obvious that such activity correctly belonged to the new Technology Consultancy Centre, rather than to individual faculties, and at the start of 1973, the nut and bolt unit was transferred officially to TCC. The early constraints at TCC—space, money and equipment—had been largely overcome during the first year. In 1971-2, UST had provided a small start-up subvention of 5,000 cedis (US$4,400), which increased the following year to 35,000 cedis, and was augmented by substantial assistance from Oxfam, Scottish War on Want and the Barclays Bank International Development Fund. Office space was provided centrally on the campus, and a spacious former generator house was handed over as a workshop. A centre lathe and drilling machine were purchased locally, and used equipment—two capstan lathes and a milling machine—arrived from Britain. The following year, grants from the Rockefeller Brothers Fund and the World Council of Churches permitted the purchase of additional equipment, so that by 1974, TCC had a reasonably well equipped and functioning machine shop. Support staff were hired locally, technical assistance was provided by various faculties and by the short-term visitors' programme of the Inter University Council of London, and a small number of skilled and highly adaptable volunteers were assigned to TCC by the US Peace Corps and the British Voluntary Service Overseas.

Nuts and bolts had become the first 'production unit' and by April 1973, monthly output had risen to a remarkable 2,000 sets, with five young apprentices from Suame learning the technique. The second production section was the Plant Construction Unit which tackled the problem of small-scale soap production. In 1972, the Government had made an effort to encourage local soapmakers to form co-operatives which could facilitate both the purchase of raw materials, and marketing. A group of soapmakers approached TCC and requested assistance in the development of a larger soap boiling tank, and when the Ministry of Industries learned of TCC's experiments, it made a grant of over 24,000 cedis, which was matched by Oxfam Quebec, to assist in the establishment of a pilot soap plant on the campus. The slippery nature of soap production in Ghana is the story of appropriate technology in

Nuts being produced from mild steel construction rod in Suame Magazine.

16

microcosm, and is worthy of a book in itself. Chapter 9 outlines the lengthy TCC experience in greater detail, but, in brief, in September 1973, when the first bars of soap were cut from the first production batch—half a ton of soap produced in 300-gallon electrically heated rectangular tanks designed and manufactured at TCC—a major step forward had been taken.

The rationale for campus production units was straight-forward. While it was not particularly difficult for skilled, trained professors to identify a solution to a technical problem, it was another matter to persuade a group or an entrepreneur to adopt the new technology or product. Skill development, dubious markets, lack of equipment or reluctance to invest in the face of uncertain profitability all conspired against the transfer of technology. These problems have plagued all appropriate technology centres over the years, and TCC's production units were an early attempt to overcome the problem in Ghana. The units could train both craftsmen and managers over a period of time while product development was completed under actual production, rather than experimental conditions. The market, too, could be tested over time and against realistic production costs, during which entrepreneurs could determine for themselves the viability of the activity. The production units were an attempt to avoid what John Powell had seen elsewhere: 'appropriate' products and tech-nologies developed but not transferred; professors acting as curators, leading visitors, especially visitors with money, past an array of rusting artifacts that would never leave the campus.

Gradually, clients from both government and the private sector began to arrive at TCC requesting assistance. A furniture manufacturer came with an urgent request for metal tube inserts to substitute for imports that had not arrived. Because the outside diameter required machining to a close tolerance, the insert became TCC's first effort in precision engineering, and 1,000 were successfully produced. The Ministry of Health asked for assistance in repairing and rehabilitating the air conditioning plant at Accra's Korle Bu Hospital. The plant had lain idle since 1965, and although it took engineers and students from various faculties nearly three years, the job was successfully completed in 1975. Feeder road studies were undertaken on behalf of the local government administration, and dozens of small entrepreneurs arrived with requests for assistance in the production of glue, leather, rubber mouldings, wood and coconut charcoal, alcohol, typewriter ribbons and even gunpowder. Some of the requests were handled by TCC, others were farmed out to relevant faculties on campus, and some were sent to ITDG in London for advice on the selection of appropriate techniques and equipment.

Even the thorny problem of consultancy fees seemed to have been overcome with an agreement that after expenses, 70 per cent of any fee would revert to the faculty member involved, 15 per cent would go to the consultant's department, and 15 per cent would be retained by TCC. Consultancy earnings were small in TCC's first two years of operation, but rose to almost 50,000 cedis (US$43,500) in 1974–5. That year, TCC's total income exceeded a quarter of a million cedis.

These were the halcyon days of intermediate technology. Voluntary agencies, long critical of 'top-down' development, were flocking to the concept, and more were added to the list of TCC's original supporters. Visitors from bilateral and UN agencies were beginning to pay calls on the production units, and when E.F. Schumacher's book, *Small Is Beautiful*, appeared in 1973,[2] it reflected perfectly what TCC was attempting to do. Schumacher followed in the honourable tradition of thinkers and writers who feared for the future of society—Mill, Huxley, Orwell, Rachel Carson, Galbraith; and of others who had proposed and lived alternatives—Thoreau at Walden Pond, Gandhi, Nyerere. 'Making use of the best of modern knowledge and experience,' Schumacher wrote, 'is conducive to decentralization, compatible with the laws of ecology, gentle in its use of scarce resources, and designed to serve the human person instead of making him the servant of machines. I have named it intermediate technology to signify that it is vastly superior to the primitive technology of bygone ages but at the same time much simpler, cheaper and freer than the super-technology of the rich. One can also call it self-help technology, or democratic or people's technology—a technology

18

to which everyone can gain admittance and which is not reserved to those already rich and powerful.'[3] The Aquarian Age had begun and the Technology Consultancy Centre had arrived. Or so it seemed.

CHAPTER 3

The Night of the Scorpion

Ghana may have been poised on the edge of a new era in 1972, but it was not one of peace and prosperity. The next dozen years would be the most difficult in the country's history, and each succeeding year would be worse than the one before. The elected government of Kofi Busia was overthrown by a military coup in 1972, and there would be two more coups before the establishment of a new civilian government and a Third Republic in 1979. The Third Republic was the briefest yet, replaced by another military regime at the end of 1981.

The economy suffered from cyclical problems and each revolution, like the turn of a screw, led to further decline. Hard currency was already in short supply in the early 1970s, and despite a brief improvement in the price of cocoa, when the first oil crisis hit in 1973, foreign exchange virtually disappeared. Decreasing investment in the export sector led to concomitant declines in the production of cocoa, timber, gold, bauxite and diamonds. And Ghana continued to pay the price for some of the earlier capital-intensive investments. Industrial goals had in many cases vastly exceeded the managerial, technological and financial resources available, and political interference only exacerbated the problem. Many import substitution enterprises, established at the expense of investment in the traditional export sector, were found to offer few real advantages when the costs were added up. One study showed that the foreign exchange costs for 15 out of 34 products studied was greater than if they had simply been imported, and using a shadow rate of exchange for the cedi, eight actually showed a negative value added.

Economic horror stories like this might have been reversed had such enterprises operated at full capacity, but given their dependence upon a hybrid pre-industrial economy and on imported raw materials and technology, the chances of this happening had probably always been non-existent. And now, manufacturing too was starved of both raw materials and spare parts for preventive maintenance and repair. Production declined and prices rose. Nevertheless, between 1972 and 1977, between 42 per cent and 55 per cent of the available foreign exchange was still sopped up by the industrial sector, 95 per cent of it for imports of industrial materials and the balance for spares and accessories. Gradually, the informal sector took over from the formal; in the motor industry, all parts, smuggled or otherwise, found their way to Suame and its equivalents in other cities and towns. Eventually the mechanics and technicians followed, and Suame Magazine grew, along with inflation and *kalebule*. By 1982, gross output in the industrial sector—manufacturing, mining, electricity, water and construction—was 52 per cent of what it had been in 1975. The average rate of capacity utilization, which may have been as high as 60 per cent in the early 1970s, had plummeted a decade later to 25 per cent or less. Manufacturing, which in 1970 had accounted for 14 per cent of GDP, had fallen by 1983 to just over 3 per cent. The devastating losses of both private and public equity capital were matched by an equally frightening loss of skilled manpower, heading for Europe and North America in their thousands, and for neighbouring West African countries in their hundreds of thousands.

Roughly 75 per cent of the cost of road building and maintenance in Ghana involves foreign exchange, and so this too declined, as did maintenance of the railway. A shortage of spares and bad roads led to a rapid deterioration of the country's now irreplaceable vehicle fleet, and to a fast-growing inability to move manufactures and produce both to local markets and to ports for export. In 1983, an estimated 70 per cent of Ghana's 92,000 heavy-duty vehicles were off the road, 40 per cent for want of tyres. Those that were serviceable rarely moved, because there was often no petrol or diesel fuel, even through the heavily controlled ration system.

In attempts to halt the slide, successive governments instituted ever more draconian price controls, further reducing output. Cocoa production plummeted while world prices stagnated and the rate of return to the actual farmer declined. The 1983 price to the cocoa producer was, in real terms, 39 per cent of what it had been in 1970. Tobacco was worth 56 per cent of the 1970 price, and cotton was a mere 34 per cent. Farmers responded as might be expected: cocoa production declined from a high of 560,000 tons to 158,000 tons in 1983–4, and Ghana's share of the world market dropped from 30 per cent in 1970 to just over 10 per cent. Tobacco fell from an average annual production of 2,700 tons to 500 tons in 1983, and cotton dropped from a 1977 high of 11,363 tons, to only 502 tons in 1983. The cedi was, by now, vastly overvalued, shifting incentives from exports to the import trade, from cocoa to subsistence farming, from production to trading and smuggling. The misallocation and misuse of import licences led to even further 'inefficiencies'. A 140 per cent devaluation in 1978 pegged the cedi at 2.75 to the US dollar, but by 1983 the unofficial rate had soared to 160, while the minimum daily wage remained at 23 cedis. The 'trickle down' approach had failed. It had proven as ineffective as what John Kenneth Galbraith once ridiculed as the 'the horse and sparrow theory': if you feed a horse enough oats, some will pass through to the road for the sparrows.

It may be thought that this critical assessment is overly harsh, but it is milder than what one hears in Ghana from ordinary Ghanaians, and it is no more sobering than the government's own assessment of past failures. Nevertheless, internal mismanagement and dubious policy choices do not account for all the problems. As noted above, the massive oil price increase of 1973 took a tremendous toll. Nature, too, conspired against Ghana in its distress. A two-year drought began in 1975, and an even more devastating one straddled the planting and harvests of 1982 and 1983. One observer who drove the 650 kilometres from Tamale to Accra on a single day in 1983 said there was hardly a moment when brush fires could not be seen; everywhere there was the pall of smoke, and it seemed as if the entire country was on fire. Precious cocoa plants, which take years to bear, and standing crops alike were destroyed.

If bad policy decisions and malign nature were not enough

22

to try the admirable resilience and renowned good humour of Ghanaians, the world economy again intervened. Except for slight improvements in 1974 and 1977, Ghana's terms of trade deteriorated steadily. The London spot price of cocoa declined from £2,935 per ton in 1977 to £1,127 in 1981. The second oil crisis in 1979 added to the burden: while Ghana's net import of petroleum products declined in volume by 9 per cent between 1979 and 1980, the cost increased by a staggering 71 per cent. International aid agencies fell away, while loans for earlier projects, by now mostly defunct, came due. In 1983, the Government of Nigeria, suffering from a recession of its own, precipitously announced the immediate expulsion of all illegal aliens, including vast numbers of Ghanaians who had migrated over the years to greener pastures. Within a matter of days, an estimated *one million* Ghanaians had returned home, further adding to the economic misery. Although many drifted back to Nigeria, they found themselves expelled once more in 1985, and the hardship entailed in resettling hundreds of thousands of people was repeated.

Inflation has been a fact of life in most countries over the past decade or so, but even in Third World terms, Ghanaians endured greater hardship than most. While Western nations were wrestling double digit inflation into single digit proportions, Ghanaians were living with triple digit figures. Table 1 shows how stark the reality was over a six-year period, especially for the rural population which bore the brunt of it.

What this meant at the end of 1984, when the official minimum wage was about to be doubled to 70 cedis a day, was that

Table 1
Consumer Price Index[1]

	1978	1979	1980	1981	1982	1983
National Combined Index	173	267	401	868	1062	2367
Urban	171	256	363	800	977	2102
Rural	174	278	448	938	1149	2457
Accra	169	276	377	772	990	1877

(Annual Average; 1977=100)

23

tomatoes were sold in Accra for 65 cedis per kg, plantain for 39 cedis, cassava for 15 cedis, and beef for an incredible 264 cedis per kg. A single egg, which in 1977 had cost 35 pesewas—the long forgotten decimal of the cedi—now cost 11 cedis, a thirtyonefold increase.

When salaries are worthless, people become corrupt. 'Ghanaians are magicians', is the explanation given for the lack of obvious starvation, but people were hungry. Salaried employees took second and third jobs; children worked; everyone planted—not the cash crops which the government managed so badly, but fruit and vegetables which could be eaten or bartered. Some stole; most hoarded; probably everyone cheated. By 1982, the government of Ghana had become inexorably separated from its people, acting like a switchboard without connections; the lights blinked, but the wires led nowhere and the interaction between force and order, delicate in any society, had completely collapsed.

The downward spiral in Ghana's economy provided the Technology Consultancy Centre with an unexpected though not altogether welcome upward twist in activity. The production units had been originally conceived as prototype manufacturing plants which, in demonstrating the viability of a product or process, were supposed to be emulated by entrepreneurs or groups in the private and non-governmental sector. With the growing shortage of foreign exchange and the increasing difficulty in obtaining spare parts, components and raw materials, there was an upswing in the number of clients appearing at the TCC door. By and large, however, they were looking for TCC to provide them with the missing element in their own production rather than the technology needed to produce it themselves. This was particularly true of the Steel Bolt Production Unit, the Metal Products Design Unit and the Plant Construction Unit, which were becoming more and more established as support and supply groups to small-scale industries that were no longer able to rely on external suppliers for badly needed components. In the view of TCC, the manufacture of steel bolts—using a simple process, locally available material, and machinery that was readily available in Suame Magazine, should have been one of the obvious success

24

stories of the first years. And yet by 1976, after four years of successful and lucrative campus production and the training of more than a dozen apprentices from Suame, not a single workshop anywhere else had taken up the production of nuts and bolts.

Sticky business

TCC had also been disappointed by the uptake on its advisory activities. Many individuals came to the campus with technical problems which were solved, often after expensive, time-consuming experimentation and even occasional reference to the Intermediate Technology Development Group in Britain. However, TCC found afterwards, to its great disappointment, that much of the advice was simply ignored. And even where there were cases of a positive transfer in technology, other factors conspired against complete success. One of the Centre's most spectacular early projects—Spider Glue—epitomized for TCC almost every issue it would face in the development and transfer of appropriate technology, and provided invaluable lessons that would be applied in future projects.

Ostensibly, Spider Glue was exactly the sort of collaboration between the university and small-scale industry that TCC had been set up to provide. In 1972, not long after the Centre began operating, a Mr S.K. Baffoe arrived seeking advice. He was a small-scale manufacturer of cassava starch in a village on the southern outskirts of Kumasi, not far from the university. He remembered making glue from cassava starch as a student at school, but found in his subsequent experiments that it had a limited shelf life, growing mouldy after a few days. TCC placed the problem before a professor in the Department of Chemistry who began to examine non-toxic preservatives, and, in anticipation of success, Baffoe was urged to obtain trial orders from stores in town. That was in March 1972. By August, the chemistry professor had found a non-toxic fungicide that would act as a preservative, as well as other additives that would make the glue waterproof. TCC helped Baffoe prepare a loan application to the bank, which included a

25

breakdown of manufacturing requirements, a cash-flow projection, and even sample bottles and labels. A 3,000 cedi overdraft followed in short order, and soon Baffoe was in production.

That November, TCC operated a stand at a 'Made in Ghana' exhibition held in Kumasi, and among the products displayed was S.K. Baffoe's Spider Glue. Visiting officials of the Ghana State Publishing Corporation, the primary distributor of stationery products in Ghana, expressed interest in the glue, and almost immediately began discussing the potential with Baffoe. By February the following year, Baffoe had obtained a certificate of approval from the Ghana National Standards Board, and not long afterwards signed an agreement with the State Publishing Corporation to supply it with 20,000 cedis (US$17,400) a month worth of Spider Glue. By the middle of 1974, Baffoe's first loan had been paid off and he had taken another in order to expand production. He was now making more than 30,000 bottles a month, employing 30 people in the village and was producing a satisfactory glue at less than a third of the import cost. In fact, his costs could have been further reduced had the development of a local bottle and spreader been possible. The government, understandably impressed with Spider Glue, moved to protect the burgeoning industry by banning the importation of glue in 1975. By then, Baffoe was making a profit of about 70,000 cedis a year on a turnover of 240,000 cedis, while at the same time saving the country an estimated 120,000 cedis (US$104,000) annually in foreign exchange.

Spider Glue seemed the ideal marriage of campus and community, an example of the right technology at the right time in the right place. A relatively uncomplicated technical and commercial input from TCC, and a small capital investment had created jobs and led to significant foreign exchange savings for Ghana. Mr Baffoe benefited, his village benefited, Ghana benefited. But once the success story seemed firmly in place, the problems began.

Perhaps fittingly, S.K. Baffoe had named his product after Ananse, the fabled spider of Ghanaian legend. The Ananse stories, which found their way intact to the Caribbean with the slave trade, were adapted in America and gradually transformed into the tales of Uncle Remus, in which Ananse, the spider, became Br'er Rabbit. Ananse, like Br'er Rabbit, is a trickster who spins a tangled web and lives on his wits, trusting no one beyond his immediate family, and for good reason. In a way, Spider Glue became for S.K. Baffoe a bit like Br'er Rabbit's tar baby: after his initial success, every move he made trapped him more and more in a sticky mess. The first disaster struck when his foreman, the only person at the factory who knew the formula for Spider Glue, ran away and set up his own glue factory. Then a chemist at the National Standards Board, who was responsible for testing and certifying the glue, set up his own nephew in glue production, withheld the renewal of Baffoe's certificate, and actually published an announcement in the newspapers stating that Spider Glue had failed to pass inspection. The lucrative orders from the State Publishing

Spider glue: an ideal marriage of campus and community; then the problems began.

27

Corporation dried up, production ceased and the jobs in Baffoe's village disappeared. Meanwhile, at the university, feelings ran high against TCC for helping an outsider to become rich, while the professor who had produced the formula had received virtually no recompense. TCC was obliged to take out expensive international patents on the formula, but as Mr Baffoe had discovered, what is correct, or fair, or even legal, does not always prove to be enforceable.

A number of salient lessons had been learned, not least by S.K. Baffoe. Eventually, through a combination of guile, gifts and righteous outrage, he succeeded—years later—in obtaining a new certificate as well as an apology from the Standards Board, and by the time of his death in 1983, he had started production again under a new brand-name. But there would never be the profits or the monopoly he had enjoyed before, and today there are probably half a dozen or more small manufacturers of glue using the TCC Spider Glue formula in Ghana. For TCC, that part of the outcome was certainly gratifying: a simple, labour-intensive technology had indeed been transferred, with all the concomitant benefits in job creation and foreign-exchange substitution. The success had been due to several factors: the local availability of raw materials, a simple technology that was only a step removed from Mr Baffoe's cassava starch production and his remembrance of gluemaking at school; there was an established market for glue, and the technology that was developed allowed Baffoe to produce at a low enough price that his product was an attractive alternative to the imported glue, yet high enough to ensure for him the return he sought on his investment.

For TCC, all these lessons were important. TCC also began to realize, as did professors who had seen the Centre as a potential money-spinner, that appropriate technology was not really going to augment personal incomes, and from the mid-1970s, earnings from consultancy work for individual faculty members declined and all but disappeared. It was becoming clear that those who needed TCC's service most were not the type of people who could pay such fees. Even Mr Baffoe, wealthy as he so briefly became, could not have afforded expensive consulting fees at the beginning. Conversely, people who could afford to pay consulting fees did not need TCC. But perhaps the most salient lesson for TCC, despite the vicissitudes of S.K. Baffoe, was that for a product or a technology to become successful in the minefield of the commercial world, it would have to be pursued by an individual or individuals who knew that world, and who possessed equal amounts of drive and initiative, both in large quantities.

Against the grain

An equally vital lesson was learned in TCC's early days regarding the initiation of projects and their dependence upon sources of supply. It had come to the attention of TCC in 1974 that the two breweries in Kumasi, large consumers of barley, were dumping as much as 120 tons of spent grain every week in the bush, where it was allowed to rot. Brewers' spent grain is a source of animal feed in many industrialized and Third World countries, and TCC decided to investigate the possibility of putting what the breweries were actually paying to discard, to good use. Analysis in the Biochemistry Department revealed that while the spent grain contained about 75 per cent water and began to ferment within 24 hours, it could be stored for long periods of time if the water content could be lowered to 12 per cent. The trick would be to reduce the moisture quickly enough to retard the fermenting process, and so a two-stage technology was developed. First, a press was constructed which reduced moisture content to 50 per cent. Various sun-drying techniques were tested, and it was found that a concrete slab, with walls painted white to increase the reflection of the sun, could do the job in about four hours. In tests at the university's Department of Animal Production, it was learned that by substituting dried spent grain for 20 per cent of the poultry feed, egg production increased by 10 per cent.

In the meantime, TCC had been approached by a man who was looking for a useful enterprise in which to invest his savings. Moses Offei knew little about brewers' spent grain, or animal feed for that matter, but he and his wife, who was a trader, were interested in the idea. Offei followed the trials at

29

the university with interest and obtained a site where he could undertake some tests of his own. TCC loaned him an improved press, made from galvanized sheet steel to replace the original model constructed from a perforated oil drum, and it was agreed that if he was satisfied after three months, he would purchase the equipment. Although initial sales were slow, they were steady enough to justify the investment, and over the next 18 months, Moses Offei bought three more presses from TCC. In his operation, he employed eight people which, at a total investment of less than 7,000 cedis for presses, floor and incidentals, amounted to 900 cedis or less than US$800 per work-place. TCC began further experiments with kerosene and electric dryers, as it was thought that solar drying would have limited application during the rainy season, although this turned out not to be the case.

In 1976, as Moses Offei was expanding his production, the Guinness brewery, seeing the market that had now been established, decided to process its own spent grain for sale to farmers. While this did not ultimately affect Offei's production, because of his price advantage and different markets, it offered an interesting comparison between competing capital-intensive and intermediate technologies. Guinness had several

Brewers' spent grain drying in the sun.

advantages, the main one being its existing boilers which could be used to produce steam heat for dehydration without requiring any additional drying equipment. A further advantage was that the brewery had been established to work on a three-shift basis, which gave it a comparative overhead advantage and the capability of handling 12 tons of wet barley a week, compared with Offei's capacity of about one-tenth that amount. Nevertheless, Offei's great advantage was in the cost of energy—for him, the sun was free—and in the end, his cost was 41 per cent less than that of the brewery. Although the Ghanaian breweries were among the last to suffer from foreign-exchange difficulties, they, too, were eventually forced to reduce production, and on a single-shift comparison, Moses Offei had a cost advantage of more than 70 per cent. Using 1975 prices, one study[2] showed that the solar drying technique provided a 59 per cent return on capital, while a further comparison in 1978[3] showed a 156 per cent return on capital, compared with 115 per cent to the brewery on a three-shift basis, a return which dropped to only 29 per cent on a single-shift basis.

What damaged Moses Offei's operation, however, was not competition from higher, more costly technology, but from something more basic, both in terms of technology and human nature. Another entrepreneur who had been watching Offei's operation decided to go into business for himself. Instead of finding or constructing a building, he dried his spent grain on a disused section of highway. Despite Offei's delivery arrangements with the brewery, Offei discovered that drivers were susceptible to his competitor's financial blandishments. And although Offei's competitor ordered a press from a shop in Suame Magazine, he never used it, as he found that he could sell his lower quality—but lower cost—product without difficulty to farmers who were increasingly desperate to find a substitute for animal feed that was by now disappearing from the market. Soon others were doing the same thing, and Offei's price was no longer competitive.

In the end, Moses Offei and his wife probably made the return on their investment that they had hoped for, and TCC could take satisfaction in the knowledge that over 6,000 tons of spent grain that had once been dumped in the bush every year was now finding a productive use. But once again, a lesson had been learned about the transfer of technology. In this case, it had not been transferred adequately, in that no specialist grain-drying industry had been established, except by Guinness. The real potential of the project had, in a sense, been subverted by a hijacker who could, in the whirlpool of the Ghanaian economy, easily substitute profit for quality. Although S.K. Baffoe's glue had been hijacked, the quality had not been, because while there was an established demand, as for animal feed, the raw material—cassava in the case of glue—was limitless, locally available and cheap. Brewers' spent grain was derived from an imported product, its supply was limited, and its availability was dependent not only on the willingness of a small number of large foreign firms to supply it, but on the grace and favour of those charged with delivering it.

TCC also concluded that it had approached the selection of the client in the wrong way. Moses Offei had been looking for something to invest in; unlike S.K. Baffoe, he had not come to TCC with a need to develop or improve a product he was familiar with. Offei did not have first-hand experience of the market-place and, despite all the cost-benefit analyses and cash flow projections, neither did TCC. In fact, if TCC had been able to identify Offei's eventual competitor earlier, he might have been the one who could have developed the specialized, high quality industry that was anticipated. TCC had made the error, all too common in the enthusiasm of new and obviously good ideas, of *persuading* someone to take the risk. This mistake was an important lesson, one that would hold fast in the coming years. Rarely again would TCC attempt to persuade anyone to take on a process or a product. By the late 1970s, when the TCC approach to clients had more fully matured, the Centre would find itself so busy with people who wanted its assistance, that there would be no time to chase people with a limited interest in brilliant ideas conceived and maintained in an artificial environment.

Baubles, bangles, bright shiny beads

In the mid 1970s, TCC became involved in a number of projects related to traditional handicrafts—weaving, pottery, wood carving, brass casting by the lost-wax method. The one which taught the most useful lesson, however, was a project in 1975 which aimed to improve the production of glass beads. Men in several villages north-west of Kumasi specialize in making a particular type of bead, which, worn on the wrist or around the waist, is not only decorative, but depending upon the colour and design, conveys a particular meaning. 'When your eyes are red, they do not sparkle,' implies one configuration; 'Difficult to live with you,' another. The beads, of which there are upwards of 60 varieties, are made from broken glass—beer bottles for green, stout bottles for brown and milk of magnesia for blue.

Other colours, especially the brighter, more sought-after ones, were originally produced from imported Italian beads. The process of manufacture is time consuming, but straight-forward. The broken glass is finely ground and then poured into tiny, cylindrical clay moulds, with cassava stalks in the centre to create a hole in the finished bead. The moulds are then baked in a wood-fired kiln at a temperature which causes sintering, or fusing, rather than melting, and which results in a unique appearance and texture in the finished bead. The beads are in great demand throughout southern Ghana and their manufacture provides livelihood for several thousand villagers, mostly men, while the marketing is, in large part, handled by women.

By 1975, as foreign exchange became more and more scarce, the first Ghanaian producers to suffer were those in small rural industries, and for the beadmaking villages, the livelihood of thousands was at stake. Beads that were reminiscent only of beer bottles and milk of magnesia would not suffice, and so the 'informal' market came into play. The much prized, hard-to-get Italian beads were now smuggled in from the Ivory Coast and Togo. Informal or black markets—*kalebule*—can be effective, but they are costly, and the price of beads soared while sales, and therefore production, declined.

33

When TCC came across the villages' problem in its survey of rural industries, it saw a simple way to assist. If the villagers had access to imported pigment—an inexpensive and readily available substance outside Ghana—they could achieve former levels of production or better, and the cost would decline, as would smuggling. In 1976, a small quantity of pigment was ordered by TCC and delivered to Dabaa, the largest of the villages, where, as in four smaller nearby villages, almost all of the men were engaged in beadmaking. The result was an immediate success; brilliantly coloured beads emerged from the moulds and all thought of smuggled Italian imports was gone forever. The people of Dabaa, Asamang and several other villages asked for more pigment, and TCC approached one of its earliest supporters, Oxfam Quebec, for assistance.

In the meantime, rather than become involved with thousands of individual beadmakers, TCC had suggested that the villagers form themselves into a co-operative. It was felt that as a co-operative, they would have more appeal to foreign donors, but more importantly, they might develop the cohesion necessary to persuade the government ultimately to grant an import licence for pigment once the 'aid' period had passed. TCC also hoped that women might be brought into the production of beads, that collectively the group might be able to purchase a mechanical polisher, and that as a co-operative they could improve the marketing of their products, perhaps even to other countries. When the 810 kg of Oxfam Quebec pigment arrived, it was repackaged in small amounts and sold by TCC to co-operative members at roughly double the cost price. The pricing rationale was an effort to establish a fund that would eventually enable the co-operatives to purchase other equipment, and far from being a burden, the prices were a welcome relief to the beadmakers after the exorbitant Italian beads. Although Dabaa, Asamang and a couple of other villages formed co-operatives, some of the smaller ones were unable to do so, and even in Dabaa, splinter groups formed. Nevertheless, TCC continued to distribute the pigments to identified co-operatives and group leaders, and was successful in obtaining a second Oxfam Quebec consignment of 1,360 kg in 1978.

About 35 beads are fired in each of these clay moulds.

In 1980, TCC convinced the government of the project's worth, and obtained, in its own name but on behalf of the co-operatives, an import licence for a ton of pigment, which reached Kumasi in May 1981. It was then that the problems began to appear. Two TCC staff were approached and offered 100,000 cedis (over US$36,000 at the prevailing exchange rate), if they would divert half the incoming shipment. Villagers in Asamang accused TCC of dealing with middlemen, claiming that pigments which were supposed to sell at 25 cedis per kg were being sold to them at as much as 500 cedis per kg. Violence was threatened. It was said that two men from Asamang had made so much money out of the pigment trade that they had been flying to London themselves in order to purchase supplies. A TCC investigation subsequently revealed that black-marketing in pigment had probably started as early as 1977, through the creation of phoney co-operatives and 'ghost' villages, through village 'leaders' who claimed to be co-operatively inclined, and individuals posing convincingly as representatives of the National Council on Women and Development. It appeared that much of the illicit trade had been conducted by the beadmakers themselves, who stood to earn much more through the sale of pigment than through the sale of beads. Probably a quarter of all the pigment imported, if not more, had been marked up through various middlemen who held villagers to ransom for the precious material. As John Powell later wrote,[4] 'In retrospect, it was realized that what happened was probably inevitable. Young and inexperienced graduates and accounts clerks were no match for the *kalebule* system which engulfed every money-making opportunity in the local economy. It was impossible to circumvent a system of which everybody was potentially a member . . . Once out of the ivory tower, the academic plunges into the real world of commerce, in which he is inevitably a novice. But he is a novice trained to learn from his experiences. The TCC emerged a sadder but wiser institution with a better understanding of the real world and a clearer definition of its own role.'

When TCC withdrew from beadmaking, a number of positive changes had taken place in the industry. The villages north of Kumasi were still in the beadmaking business, producing more, brighter and better quality beads than ever before. The importation of pigments, the price of which had dropped significantly following the investigation and the establishment of an open market, had replaced the costlier practice of importing expensive, finished Italian beads, either formally or informally. TCC put some of the problems down to its naivety in ignoring advisers who said that it was wrong to subsidize pigments, or any other scarce commodity. Only by allowing market forces to find their own levels, especially in an economy as stricken as Ghana's, would a project demonstrate its viability. And in a country where co-operatives had a notoriously poor success rate, TCC had learned its own lesson, further sharpening its notion of what made an appropriate client: groups that came together at the instigation of an external agent, regardless of incentive, were unlikely to have the cohesion, the internal trust, or the drive to be more than passive actors in the development process.

The weaver's trade

In 1972, long before it became involved with the beadmaking villages, TCC had taken an interest in the potential for expansion of the rural weaving industry. As with beadmaking, certain villages in southern Ghana concentrate almost exclusively on weaving, and around Kumasi there were several where the main output was traditional kente cloth. Highly distinctive in their elegant blues, yellows, greens and reds, their unique ribbed texture and weight, various kente patterns take on different meanings, not the least of which is an indication of the wealth and importance of the owner. Woven exclusively by men and boys on narrow looms four to seven inches in width,

The metal broadloom developed at TCC had none of the taboos for women associated with the narrow kente loom.

37

the finished strips are sewn together to produce, among other things, the traditional Ghanaian male 'cloth', reminiscent of a voluminous Roman toga. In contrast with the kente villages, huge capital-intensive textile mills had been established in Accra and other urban centres over the years, flooding the market with a variety of locally produced cloth of varying quality and cost. Highly dependent on both imported cotton and yarns, as well as foreign exchange for spares and maintenance, the output from the textile mills was, by the early 1970s, already facing a downward slide, although the extent of the decline could hardly have been predicted at the time.

TCC's interest lay in identifying a technology somewhere between the traditional and the high-speed loom. Observation of kente weavers indicated that production could be increased by the introduction of a hand-operated broadloom, and so, producing a modified copy of a 40-inch English broadloom in conjunction with the university's College of Art, TCC fielded a model on a three-month trial basis to a village kente weaver. His approval and subsequent purchase of the loom led to the purchase of four more by a Catholic vocational school for girls in northern Ghana, and TCC embarked on the production of a further 20 looms through a local workshop, in the expectation that more orders would be forthcoming. Except for the reed, all parts were locally constructed, and eventually even a successful reed was made locally from bamboo. Despite the availability of reasonably priced looms, however, and a well-attended course on broadloom weaving offered by the College of Art, few individuals came forward with requests for looms, and it was decided that a temporary Weaving Production Unit should be started on campus, in conjunction with the Department of Industrial Art. Like the other production units, the aim was to test the reliability of the looms and the economic viability of the cloth under production conditions. It would also serve as a training facility, and, most importantly, in its demonstration effect, it might persuade entrepreneurs or traditional weavers to take up the new loom for their own operations.

The general outcome was disappointing, although there was

one obvious success. Unlike other projects where tradition, superstition, or simple, unreconstructed human nature had impeded the acceptance of a new idea, TCC discovered that the broadloom opened a sudden new opportunity for women. Kente weaving was forbidden to women because of an ancient belief that they would become barren if they worked the narrow loom, but there was no proscription regarding the unknown broadloom. As a result, attendance at weaving courses was shared equally by men and women, and thanks to the introduction of the first four TCC looms, broadloom training programmes were expanded at vocational schools for girls in the north.

While many of the trainees undoubtedly found employment as weavers, however, and 75 broadlooms were sold to trainees or to the private sector over the years, the numbers were significantly less than had been anticipated, and the campus production unit itself usually ran at a considerable loss. Some of this was put down to inadequate supervision, for, by 1978, the cloth was generally of good quality and customers were never in short supply. A further explanation, however, lay in the possibility that cottage industry broadloom weaving—a potentially viable proposition in 1972—was simply not feasible in the deteriorating economy of the late 1970s. Neither weavers nor entrepreneurs were interested in making an investment which could not show an early and reasonable return.

'Reasonable' return, a concept which excites much controversy among economists in Ghana, is a subject which has been pondered at length by TCC. One economist studying TCC's nut and bolt operation believed that unless a potential small-scale investor could be assured of a 40 per cent return on capital, productive enterprises were unlikely to be more attractive than simple trading. While such a high rate of return might be unreasonable elsewhere, it made eminent sense in the Ghana of the late 1970s and early 1980s. With a vastly undervalued cedi and government restrictions on almost anything that impinged on local production, emphasis had been diverted from cash crops and small-scale industry to subsistence farming and an import sector characterized to a large extent by the black market and smuggled goods. Growing scarcity in all consumer goods meant that there were immense profits to be made from trading, and the profits could be realized quickly. As with glass beads, where beadmakers substituted trade in imported pigment for production, there was little incentive for capital investment in production, unless the return was large or, as will be seen in other areas, where capital equipment would retain its value or even appreciate.

This was not the case with broadloom weaving. When the economy of Ghana reached the nadir of 1983, local cotton growing had all but ceased, and imported yarn had become unavailable except at the most exorbitant of *kalebule* prices. TCC stopped its weaving projects, although within two years of closure, a number of things had changed. Inflation had declined and income had improved somewhat in relation to prices. By 1986, it was still too early to predict whether the broadloom weaving project might be resuscitated, but the tentative beginnings of a cotton-spinning project in Tamale (described in Chapter 11) suggested new potential, with new directions based on what had been learned during the darkest days in Ghana.

Glue, brewer's spent grain, beadmaking and broadloom weaving—each project had, in its way, felt the paralyzing sting of the scorpion. These four examples represent only a small part of TCC's work during the 1970s; there were other projects, large and small, which enjoyed varying degrees of success. But all faced the same constraints within the badly listing economy, skewed by societal values, government policies and the world market. For technology development to be successful, these things had not only to be considered, they had to be uppermost in all design and planning. TCC was also gradually coming to the complementary conclusion that technology researched and developed, no matter how appropriate in theory, no matter what it had taken into consideration, was worthless unless it could attract agents within the society to take it and use it productively. Thus the *transfer* of technology gradually came to replace product research and development as the most important aspect of the work of the Technology

Consultancy Centre. It seemed a logical evolution at the time, but it was a development which would eventually set TCC very much apart from most other appropriate technology institutions in the Third World.

CHAPTER 4

The Day of the Phoenix

Studying the economy of Ghana is a bit like sitting in a small boat at night during a storm. It is hard to know whether you are on the crest of a wave or in a trough, but it is obvious that the tossing and turning amidst the spray has more to do with the wind above than with the currents below. Even when the storm has passed, it is difficult to know which waves result from the silent but inexorable movement beneath the surface and which are accidents of the wind. In Ghana, each successive government has heralded a new order, free of corruption, founded on social justice, hard work and economic growth. Despite brief periods of improvement, however, the overall decline through Ghana's first quarter century of independence was steady and steep. Reading too much, therefore, into the preliminary performance of a new government or a new policy, is fraught with peril. Nevertheless, after 1981 there were a number of changes in Ghana which significantly altered the climate in which small-scale enterprises operated, and to ignore them is to describe only part of the context in which the Technology Consultancy Centre operated in the mid 1980s.

The International Monetary Fund

The Provisional National Defence Council, which ousted the Third Republic at the end of 1981, spoke loudly against corruption and mismanagement, and talked of a revolution that would transform the social and economic order of Ghana. 'People's Defence Committees' were established throughout the country, and the tenor of politics through 1982 rang with the fervour of revolutionary rhetoric. It was a year of disorder as the government attempted to sort out the policies and confusion it had inherited. Mistakes were made and the economy at first continued on its steep descent. Then, in 1983, the government unveiled an economic recovery programme which had been developed in co-ordination with the International Monetary Fund and the World Bank.

The IMF's many critics were quick to denounce the government for having 'sold out' the revolution, but turning around or even slowing an economic decline such as the one Ghana had experienced for so long, could not happen quickly or easily. To continue the maritime metaphor, the Ghanaian economy was like a huge ocean-going freighter, already scraping bottom, whose Captain, high up on the bridge, spins the wheel, knowing that the ship will not respond for several miles. By the summer of 1985, when this book was being written, the wheel on the Ghanaian bridge had been spun, but after 18 months, the economy was just beginning to respond. The turn on the bridge had been dramatic. The cedi, long held at 2.75 to the US dollar, was devalued. The *kalebule* rate of exchange was 160 to the dollar, so even an official devaluation to 24.69 to the dollar, while as dramatic as any in Africa, was still far short of the real exchange rate. Through 1984, 1985 and 1986, further devaluations took the rate to 90 to the dollar, while the black-market rate actually dropped slightly. This in itself was an indication of some success, as often under such circumstances, the black-market rate simply adjusts itself upwards to accommodate the official change.

The second change was an attempt to establish more realistic relative prices and incomes. The cocoa farmer had long before lost any financial incentive to produce for the official market, as the control price was a fraction of what it had once been; in 1982–3, the indexed producer price of cocoa was 19 per cent of what it had been 20 years earlier. The incentive was therefore away from cocoa and towards almost anything else, or towards the 'informal export' potential. One conservative estimate suggests that 15 per cent of the country's cocoa crop in the late 1970s was being smuggled out, a reflection of the fact that the purchasing power of the return on cocoa was six times in neighbouring countries what it was in Ghana.

As part of the recovery programme, the producer price of cocoa was raised 67 per cent in 1983, and then by a further 50 per cent the following year. However it still lagged behind prices offered by smugglers. Public sector and minimum wages were increased, in an effort to offset erosion in real incomes, although wages still lagged far behind the actual cost of living. Other fiscal and monetary measures were taken, but one of the most important events was the reactivation of the long-dormant 'consultative group of donors', a group aimed at co-ordinating and optimizing the aid programmes of the largest bilateral and multilateral agencies. The IMF loaned Ghana US$355 million in 1983 and US$236 million in 1984, and the international aid community allocated a further $415 million in 1984, followed by $500 million in 1985. It was these credits, loans and grants which gave the economy the badly needed, if somewhat artificial injections of adrenalin it needed for rehabilitation programmes in key sectors of the economy.

Ghana had become something of a 'test case' in Africa for the IMF, and by the end of 1984, the country's indebtedness to the Fund was surpassed by only four other countries in Africa: the Ivory Coast, the Sudan, Zaire and Zambia. This factor notwithstanding, Ghana's total indebtedness was low by African standards; of 38 countries, only six—Burundi, Burkina Faso, Ethiopia, Rwanda, Chad and Uganda had a lower per capita debt burden.[1]

Trade liberalization meant that by 1985, long-vanished consumer goods were once again available in the market-place, but at a price which reflected the new and more realistic exchange rate. Petrol, which had been almost non-existent through 1983 and 1984, returned, and vehicles once again began to move produce to market and to port. The overall economy grew by 6 per cent in 1984, the first reversal of the downward trend since 1978, and inflation, which had been 123 per cent in 1983 and the highest in Africa for a full decade, fell to 40 per cent through 1984, and was expected to be half that in 1985. Manufacturing output increased and the value of exports grew in 1984 by 29 per cent. Arrears on short-term debt fell to their lowest point since 1977, well below what had been targeted in the IMF agreement.

Not all of the positive indicators can be put down to changes in economic policy, however. It could be said, in fact, that

44

there was nowhere for Ghana to go but up, especially after the disastrous drought and fires of 1983. Weather conditions returned to normal in 1984 and 1985, leading to improved harvests of both food and cash crops. More hydro-electric power was available because water behind the Akosombo Dam had at last risen to an acceptable level, and the world cocoa price, so long depressed, had improved. But there were storm warnings ahead. In an effort to reduce costs and tighten management in the Cocoa Marketing Board, several thousand lay-offs were declared, pitting labour and the new policies against one another. Disbursements from bilateral donor agencies, never speedy at the best of times, lagged far behind needs and hopes. Nigeria once again expelled hundreds of thousands of Ghanaians. And most problematic of all, the world cocoa price began to take a nosedive once again. September 1985 deliveries traded at £1,720 a ton, £500 less than the seven-year high established only months earlier.

Cocoa is, of course, the classic case of Third World single-commodity dependence, and Ghana has often been cited as the prime example of a country victimized by the existing world economic order, mercilessly bound, after nearly three decades of independence, to a colonial export crop. Nkrumah recognized the problem, and his solution, not unreasonable in theory, was that Ghana should industrialize. His government and most of those that followed, ignored cocoa and pumped the revenue and foreign exchange it produced into an industrial infrastructure that never paid off. As a result, less and less cocoa was produced, and increasingly fewer alternatives were available to government, while the goose that had laid the golden egg became progressively more sick.

Another alternative commonly offered to dependence on a single commodity is the idea that countries like Ghana should concentrate on food production and self-sufficiency instead of wasting their life's blood on export crops that will probably always lag behind the cost of imports. Obviously, it is in the interest of all countries to become as self-sufficient in food production as possible; however the argument is often simplistic. Land is finite, but populations are not. Ghana, which achieved independence with fewer than seven million

45

people, is expected to have a population of 24 million by the turn of the century. Increased production ultimately means the need for more agricultural equipment, fertilizers and pesticides. There are an estimated one million small farms in Ghana where the basic tools are the hoe and cutlass; these alone, without any reference to mechanized farming, represent a large market—and demand—for steel. The desirability of organic farming notwithstanding, an infestation of stem-borers can wipe out 90 per cent of a maize crop within days if pesticide is not used. In 1981, Ghana was using 12 times more fertilizer than it had a decade earlier, but was still running a serious food deficit. Transportation was required for the movement of food, and that meant vehicles, roads and fuel, all of which required foreign exchange. In short, Ghana was a country in which a combination of bad choices and declining conditions of trade had produced a vortex from which there were few simple exits. It might be argued that Third World countries could make do with *less* foreign exchange, but the truth is that many, if not most, are already making do with much less per capita than ever before, and what they have goes a lot less far than it once did.

The same old International Economic Order

A third alternative relates to structural reform in world trade. Many eloquent Third World economists and politicians have shown how an acre's worth of jute or sisal or sugar will purchase half, a third, a quarter the number of tractors it did five or ten years ago. The same is true of cocoa, although here it is even more dramatic. Between February and September of 1985 alone, 22 per cent fewer tractors could be purchased with the same tonnage of cocoa, assuming a constant price for tractors. Over the years, there have been many proposals for internationally financed and managed commodity buffer stocks, the most comprehensive of which emerged from the Sixth Special Session of the United Nations General Assembly in 1974. The 'New International Economic Order', as it was called, was a three-fold plan. The first part was to create a fair deal for Third World commodities, which would include the establishment of buffer stocks, research and development to strengthen 16 basic Third World commodities against competition, and an indexed pricing system to protect Third World income from the ravages of inflation in industrialized countries.

A second aim was to increase the manufacturing capacity of Third World countries through the transfer of technology, the reduction of tariff and non-tariff barriers to trade, and greater control over the activities of transnational corporations. A third objective was an increase in official development assistance, ideally to levels targeted years before.

Ten years after the call for a new international economic order, little had been accomplished, and almost nothing beneficial to Ghana. The world price of cocoa was still volatile, and though world demand had remained consistent, other Third World countries, notably Brazil and Ivory Coast, had moved into the void created by Ghana's subsidence. Efforts that producer countries made to control production, and therefore reduce price fluctuations, were inconsequential. A buffer stock, created in 1983, proved to be politically unmanageable. In any case, effective use of a buffer stock might have smoothed out the peaks and troughs in world prices, but it would have done little to stem overall erosion in the value of cocoa. World trade patterns became more rather than less restrictive after the call for a new international economic order, and official development assistance faltered. By 1984, of 17 OECD nations, only five had reached the 1970 target of 0.7 per cent of GNP. For Ghana, aid inflows in the late 1970s and early 1980s were half per capita of many other sub-Saharan countries, and as will be seen in Chapter 6, the pittance that was directed towards small-scale enterprises and light engineering was a blessing of very mixed proportions. If anything, the early 1980s were marked by a harder, more selfish attitude to long-term structural problems, and by a preoccuption with the relief efforts required to deal with the symptoms of problems which might have been apprehended years before.

For Ghana, a partial solution to its problems may lie in export diversification, and in the increased production of commodities that are already well known: rubber, palm oil, coconut, cotton, tobacco and industrial tree crops. But the increase in manufacturing capacity mooted as part of the NIEO remains one of the few realistic avenues to a reduction of reliance on policies which stress the importance of foreign exchange, domestic savings and capital inflows. Given the experience of the past, however, it is unlikely that it will come about through any sudden beneficence among donors, trading partners or potential investors. The fundamental question remained in 1986 as to whether the government could create and maintain the climate and the incentives necessary for the development of technologies and products that were more appropriate than what had gone before.

CHAPTER 5

Coming of Age in Suame

In Twi, one of the major languages of Ghana, the motto of the University of Science and Technology is *Nyansapo Waseneno Dadwema*. Literally translated, it means 'a riddle is solved by a wise man', but *nyansapo* is more than a riddle; *nyansapo* is the wisdom knot, a well-known design in traditional Adinkra textile patterns, in the symbolic motifs of Ashanti stools, architecture, pottery and brass gold weights. Untying the wisdom knot is more complicated than solving a riddle; it is the entire business of life. TCC has a motto of its own: 'I must change myself and play many parts,' also derived from an old Ashanti symbol. Together, the two mottoes sum up both the need and the approach to development that was fast evolving at TCC. In order to approach the wisdom knot, change and versatility were required. As TCC began to develop a definition of appropriate technology and a methodology for its transfer, change and versatility would be required first and foremost within the Centre itself; accepted textbook notions about people, technology, and development would be challenged, tested, in some cases found wanting, and changed.

Down from the ivory tower

By 1976, it had become clear that as models from which new products and techniques would be spun off into the informal sector, the campus production units were not working. There were few off-campus broadloom weavers, fewer soapmakers and no manufacturers of nuts and bolts, despite obviously successful and viable campus demonstration units. Shortages of raw materials, a paucity of entrepreneurs and other factors played their part in this, but early suspicions of a more fundamental reason had become a certainty after four years of

49

operation: a university campus would never become the launching pad for small-scale industries in the informal sector. Many of the people TCC sought to reach were illiterate and were intimidated by the university. Most worked in villages, far from Kumasi, or across town in Suame Magazine, a place as intellectually distant from the campus as the moon. The campus was a protected environment as well, a place where water, electricity and other basic inputs required by production units could be taken for granted. There, amidst the flowering bougainvillaea and frangipani, along the broad avenues and across the rolling lawns, life was orderly, calm and usually— though not always—rational; in other words, it was unreal. It was decided, therefore, that if the informal industrialists would not come to TCC, TCC would go to them.

The proposal for off-campus Intermediate Technology Transfer Units was a simple enough idea, and once proposed, the idea took firm root. It was suggested that the first ITTU should be established in Suame, another somewhere in the north, and possibly a third in the port city of Tema. An Intermediate Technology Transfer Unit would consist of a group of basic workshops, located in an informal industrial area, operated by TCC to undertake work in blacksmithing, carpentry, sheet metal work and metal machining. Campus production units would be transferred to the ITTU, and clients would have more regular access to them for on-the-job training in a more realistic production setting. ITTU staff and engineers would be available to clients, not miles away on the campus, but close enough that ideas could be discussed, techniques developed, and experiments attempted in the client's own workshop. In getting to know its clients better, TCC would also be able to assist them with more realistic costings and cash-flow projections, and would be close enough to help when things went 'off course'. Funds might even be provided for loans to potential clients who did not have access to the formal credit system.

Had TCC known how long it would take to establish the first ITTU, or any idea of the costs in time, energy and money that would be consumed, it is probably fair to say that the idea would have been smothered at birth. Luckily, however, especially for the clients who would eventually benefit from it, the concept received warm approval, if not financing, from the university, the government, and a series of international aid agencies. The story of the establishment of the first two ITTUs is told in Chapter 6, and of how they actually work in Chapters 7 and 11; suffice it to say here that an integral part of TCC's evolving approach to technology transfer was a recognition that the focus had to be shifted away from the sanitized campus setting and located as close to the centre of the informal industrial sector as possible.

Coming to terms

The next step for TCC was to define for itself a clear notion of appropriate technology as it applied to Ghana. But before this was possible, TCC had to determine its *purpose* in developing and attempting to transfer appropriate technology. This may have seemed unnecessary, especially for an established AT institution, but development organizations occasionally lose sight of key objectives in the clash of values and politics, and in the mundane but nonetheless real need to pay salaries.

One unfortunate but not uncommon reason for Third World institutions becoming involved in appropriate technology is that some foreign aid agencies think it is a good idea. They have the funds available to promote it, and to persuade others to pursue it without developing a rationale for themselves. A second motivating factor was present in the origins of TCC—a desire by expatriates and other backyard inventors to 'do something useful'. Sadly, the Third World is littered with expensive cast-off junk produced by hobbyists who thought they were appropriate technologists. Another reason derives from the Western 'counter-culture', which sees in the appropriate technology movement an opportunity to return to a simpler time, to a less complicated, idealized lifestyle. This may be commendable in urbanized, industrialized, dehumanized consumer-oriented societies, but *returning* to simpler ways is not a useful starting point for a subsistence farmer faced with eight-foot high elephant grass and armed only with a cutlass and hoe. The Walden Pond school of appropriate technology

51

sometimes forgets that Henry David Thoreau did not head for the harsh frontier; he stayed in New England, close to his mother's kitchen and the benefits of organized society, on a path that was well beaten, not by farmers and small-scale industrialists, but by writers and intellectuals like himself.

At the Technology Consultancy Centre, the purpose of working towards the acceptance of appropriate technologies had obviously to be defined in terms of development; development of the person, development of the society, development of the nation. And in the latter half of Ghana's Second Decade of Independence, this could be more precisely defined as production—production of food; production of the tools to improve the production of food; production of the equipment needed to provide basic human needs such as water, health, clothing and housing; production that would lead to the creation of secure jobs and reasonable incomes. In a society where the production of almost everything conceivable had declined so badly, where the greatest human energy was focused on getting, and trading, rather than producing, production became the single most important guideline for the Technology Consultancy Centre. Thus, by 1976, TCC could safely say that it was in business, not to encourage appropriate technology, but *through* appropriate technology to encourage productive enterprise wherever possible. Appropriate technology was only the means to an end, not the end in itself.

Definitions and checklists in the development field are as fraught with shortcomings as all generalizations. Nevertheless, as a means of understanding where the Technology Consultancy Centre is situated in the constellation of appropriate technology organizations, how it differs from other institutions and why, consideration of some basic definitions may be useful. 'Intermediate Technology', for example, is commonly defined as a technology standing half-way between the traditional and the modern. It is a relative notion: animal traction, lying between the traditional hoe and motorized traction, is an intermediate technology in Africa, but in Asia, it is a traditional technology. 'Appropriate Technology' according to Jéquier and Blanc, is a 'generic term for a wide range of technologies characterized by any one or several of the

52

following features: low investment cost per work-place, low capital investment per unit of output, organizational simplicity, high adaptability to a particular social or cultural environment, sparing use of natural resources, low cost of final product or high potential for employment.'[1]

The terms 'appropriate' and 'intermediate technology' have, to a certain extent, been used interchangeably in this book, because at TCC little distinction is made between them: for an intermediate technology to be successfully applied in Ghana, it must have the attributes of appropriate technology. Similarly, if a technology under consideration is to be 'appropriate' to Ghana's considerable needs, it is bound to lie somewhere between the traditional and the modern. But where TCC differs from the standard definition of intermediate technology is in the suggestion that it lies half-way between the traditional and the modern. If an intermediate technology is to be appropriate, it must, in the view of TCC, follow closely on the heels of the technology that is known; to skip important stages in the learning process is as short-sighted for the society as for the individual. This is not to say that a country like Ghana is condemned to a century-long industrial revolution where every cog in every wheel must be re-invented. It does mean, however, that the most logical step between hoe and tractor may not be animal traction. It may be minimum tillage farming of the sort developed by the International Institute for Tropical Agriculture in Ibadan and introduced to Ghana in 1980 by TCC. It may be more effective planting techniques, higher yielding seed varieties, organic weed and pest control or alley cropping. It may be little more than a better hoe, made locally rather than imported, or from tempered rather than untempered steel. Similarly, the most appropriate improvement on the bullock may not be a tractor, or even a hand-operated motorized tiller, but a more efficient plough, or additional animal-powered equipment, or improved seeds and agricultural techniques.

TCC's experiences in agriculture, agro-industry and food processing all testify to the validity of the 'next stage' approach to technology development in Ghana, as will be seen in Chapter 8. The same is true of the informal industrial sector.

53

Taking time off from the hectic pace of his crowded Anloga workshop, one of TCC's earliest clients, Solomon Adjorlolo, proudly takes the visitor past the impressive range of products he now manufactures, developed over long years with the painstaking assistance of TCC: cassava graters, block presses, kernel crackers, oil presses, and a corn milling machine, something with which his younger brother and partner, Ben, is particularly pleased. After a tour of the shop, in their dark, cramped little office, Ben Adjorlolo modestly reminds the enthusiastic visitor that although their workshop is a break-through of sorts, it only represents a preliminary stage in Ghana's industrial revolution. It is, however, an important stage that cannot be skipped. 'The whole history of the development of machinery,' he says, 'can be traced to the history of the corn mill. With the invention of the corn mill, the Greek poet, Antipatros, hailed the water wheel for grinding corn as the giver of freedom.'[2] This cautious reminder of developmental and technological history, the more remarkable for its eloquence and the unlikely setting in which it is offered, epitomizes perfectly TCC's 'next stage' approach.

The same lesson applies to other TCC clients. The glue produced by S.K. Baffoe and his competitors was a logical next step from the production of cassava starch. The brewer's spent grain project can probably attribute the limitations of its success to the fact that a process much simpler than the one devised by TCC became available. When there was finally a spin-off from the nut and bolt production unit, it was not into the hands of blacksmiths, but into small shops already familiar with basic machine tools, where the manufacture of simple products was a logical progression from using the equipment solely for repair work.

Making a list and checking it twice

Most definitions and checklists on appropriate technology contain certain basic criteria; for example, an appropriate technology is:

—low in capital investment
—uses locally available materials

54

—emphasizes job creation, using local skills and labour
—is affordable to small groups
—can be understood, controlled and maintained by the intended beneficiaries
—is organizationally simple and adaptable to local circumstances
—can be locally produced, preferably at the village level.

Two additional concepts are often appended to the list of criteria, usually by 'First World' NGOs. The first is that technology should rely as much as possible on renewable energy resources such as wind, water, animal and pedal power, biogas generation and solar energy. And the second is that appropriate technology should, as much as possible, involve group or community action, rather than individual application.

Criteria like these appear at first glance to accord well with the TCC approach. There are, however, some fundamental differences that have developed out of the Ghanaian experience. For example, economic viability is a generally accepted criterion —low capital cost, local materials, small enough in scale to be affordable. But even an *affordable* product or technology is not necessarily economically viable. One of the most graphic examples of this for TCC, described in Chapter 9, is soapmaking. Dozens of soapmakers eventually adopted the TCC procedure, producing an acceptable, low cost, and definitely affordable product. Many discovered, however, that when the giant Lever Brothers plant obtained enough foreign exchange to resume production, people were willing to pay twice the price for a soap whose only evident superiority was its round shape, its perfumed scent and its attractive packaging. What the local soapmakers learned were basic lessons in elasticities of price and demand, not to mention human nature and the ubiquitous Ghanaian preference for things foreign. Demand for the affordable product declined, making its production—if we are to remain with the word affordable— unaffordable to many producers.

Profit
Rather than terms such as 'affordable' and 'economically

55

viable', TCC has centred clearly on the concept of profit. 'Profit transfers technology,' is a theme that runs through TCC reports, and it is a theme one often sees painted on the back of lorries throughout Ghana; *Sika Ne Hene*—'Money Is King'. And it is an obvious factor in the emigration of hundreds of thousands of Ghanaians, an almost unbelievable proportion of the country's talented work-force, to the economic enticements of Nigeria and beyond. The profit motive does not square easily, however, with criteria regarding collective community action, nor is it a popular concept with non-governmental aid agencies. It is absent from most literature on appropriate technology, and the idea of professors helping other people to make money horrified the University of Science and Technology, first in the case of S.K. Baffoe and in most projects thereafter.

But it was in Ghana's small-scale industry, all of it in the private sector, where the vitality and creativity and essence of the country's industrial revolution was rooted. While a quarter of the nation's manufacturing output in 1974 came from small-scale industry, it absorbed fully 81 per cent of the manufacturing labour force[3]. And although the data on small-scale industry in Ghana is uneven, two studies undertaken in the mid 1970s[4] calculated that the value added per unit of invested capital was between 3.6 and 5 times higher for small-scale industries employing fewer than nine individuals, than it was for industries employing more than 30. They further showed that the capital required to create jobs in small-scale industry in 1976 was 1,100 cedis per work-place, compared with 12,518 cedis in large industries, and that the return on capital in shops employing nine people or fewer averaged 73 per cent, while in large-scale manufacturing it was only 4 per cent.

Schumacher was highly critical of a private enterprise system in which the profit motive alone became 'the perfect measuring rod for the degree of success or failure,' where profit alone determined the viability of a particular action, and no consideration was given to whether it was 'conducive to the wealth and well-being of society, whether it leads to moral, aesthetic, or cultural enrichment.'[5] But Schumacher distinguished clearly between large corporations and small-scale

56

entrepreneurs, especially those involved in the production of goods with developmental value. 'The so-called private ownership of large-scale enterprises is in no way analogous,' he wrote, 'to the simple property of the small landowner, craftsman or entrepreneur . . . in small-scale enterprise, private ownership is natural, fruitful and just.'

He went even further, celebrating the value of the entrepreneur in the sort of antinomy—a contradiction between laws—that he enjoyed:

> 'Without order, planning, predictability, central control, accountancy, instructions to the underlings, obedience, discipline—without these things, nothing fruitful can happen, because everything disintegrates. And yet—without the magnanimity of disorder, the happy abandon, the *entrepreneurship* venturing into the unknown and incalculable, without the risk and the gamble, the creative imagination rushing in where bureaucratic angels fear to tread—without this, life is a mockery and a disgrace.'[6]

In Ghana, there is a tendency towards 'a conservative modernity', which results in what economist Maxwell Owusu called 'a weak innovative impulse among Ghanaian businessmen'. Ghana's small-scale industries, therefore, deserve much respect and admiration from those with the country's economic interests at heart, for despite the get-rich-quick lure of trading, *kalebule* and emigration, they created products and services and jobs where none existed before, and did so against tremendous political and economic odds, with little support from government and virtually none from the international community. Those that did it well were able to make two and two add up to five, or six or more, and it is probably this aspect that discomfits intellectuals and aid agencies most. Part of the problem is an ideological unhappiness with the profit motive, especially on the part of salaried individuals without personal experience of the commercial world. Part is an understandable and justifiable concern with the more rapacious elements of capitalism as practised in the Third World. And part is intellectual laziness and lack of imagination on the part of aid organizations, unable or unwilling to justify the use of charitable donations for the 'enrichment' of others.

On this latter point, TCC gradually developed an innovative formula that both satisfied the technical aspect of the criticism and doubled the value of foreign contributions. It started with the nut and bolt production unit, still firmly tied to the university. One of the biggest problems in finding an entrepreneur who could produce nuts and bolts off-campus was the fact that despite the identification of interested and potentially competent producers, none of the shops in Suame had the full range of equipment—lathe, milling machine and drill—necessary to go into production. By 1976, even if an entrepreneur had the money, the machines were no longer available in Ghana and foreign exchange could not be obtained for imports. So TCC took the unprecedented, almost desperate step of selling some of its own machines to potential manufacturers—in cedis and at market value—in order to get production started. The result was positive: although much of the success can be ascribed to TCC's careful selection of the clients, without the transfer of equipment, the transfer of nut and bolt technology might never have been achieved.

Based on this preliminary success, TCC approached several international aid agencies with the idea of importing and reselling more machine tools to small-scale entrepreneurs. The breakthrough came two years later when the Intermediate Technology Development Group allocated £20,000 for used British machine tools which could be resold to small-scale industries in Kumasi. Proceeds from the sales, in cedis, were then available to TCC for other programmes. Thus, instead of simply making a grant to TCC, the ITDG contribution had done double duty in enabling carefully selected entrepreneurs to purchase machine tools necessary for production. Once the formula had been tested and approved, other organizations such as the Canadian International Development Agency followed the ITDG lead, while the EEC and others established variations on the theme.

Choosing partners

In all of this, client selection has been of paramount importance to TCC. Essentially, there are two types of client selection which have evolved over the years. In agriculture and agro-industry, selection can proceed quickly and without attaching too much rigour to the entrepreneurial profit motive. Usually the projects and products are not large, and the amount of capital involved is small. This is not to suggest a casual approach to this sector of the economy, which will be described in greater detail in Chapter 8, rather the advantages in economies of scale. For example, TCC has been involved either directly or indirectly in the manufacture and distribution of hundreds of beehives; the care and attention required to ensure adequate support for each hive is determined first by the nature of the enterprise—in this case a relatively straight-forward technology—and secondly by the client. In the case of small rural industries such as beekeeping, soapmaking, palm oil extraction, or corn milling, the client is usually not an individual, but another agency such as the National Council on Women and Development or the National Youth Council. Sometimes an international agency will approach TCC with a bulk order for equipment, or with a request to devise and run a workshop. The National Service Secretariat which co-ordinates the two-year placement in government service of all university graduates, placed large orders for beehives and requested several workshops and follow-up visits for its people. In these cases, the client is like a sub-contractor, and because the technology has been proven, TCC has only an indirect relationship with the end user; the individual who wants a single hive or two corn mills can be referred to an implementing agency or to a TCC client like the Adjorlolo brothers who already produce the item.

On the light engineering side, however, client selection is highly rigorous, time consuming and difficult, not only because much larger amounts of money are involved, but because the technology is more sophisticated, and because the success of almost all of TCC's other work has come to depend upon the success of a manufacturing capacity in the informal industrial sector. The first, and most important factor in selecting a client in the industrial sector is time. TCC must know the individual well, and the client must understand TCC and its expectations. Many people approach TCC asking for

59

assistance in obtaining equipment, but only four or five out of a hundred will return for a second discussion. It is quickly pointed out that TCC is not a trading organization or a machine supplier; if a candidate has an idea for a product, TCC will consider how it might assist, but if the request is predicated on equipment alone, it is unlikely to succeed. Urgency will almost always kill a relationship as well, because it can take as much as two years before a partnership with TCC will bear tangible fruit.

If a request for assistance is accepted, TCC will inevitably expect to work closely with the client, evaluating existing equipment, knowledge, skills and drive. On-the-job training, often for more than a year, may be required, either for the client or for trainees from the client's shop. The anticipated product will most likely be developed at TCC and put into production, in close co-operation with the client, before any new equipment is actually ordered. The client will be given tasks which will allow TCC to determine the seriousness of his or her interest, the extent and nature of the motivation, and the limits of experience and knowledge. A market survey for the proposed product may be requested; trial orders may be required. Certainly, as the time for decision nears, the client will have to organize the financing, ancillary equipment, raw material, and possibly land and buildings for a workshop. This can entail further permissions and other demonstrations of commitment, such as the arrangement of a three-phase electrical connection, no mean feat in Kumasi.

In short, client selection is a filtering process of the most rigorous kind, through which TCC identifies and partially develops the technical and commercial talents that will be required for an individual to survive in a manufacturing context. Most clients emerge from the Suame Magazine ethic, which is very different from the TCC approach. The average Suame machine-tool owner knows that a lathe, for example, is a valuable piece of equipment that will appreciate, rather than depreciate, if it remains in good condition. The motivation, therefore, is to minimize its use, an attitude encouraged in Suame by the high demand for vehicle repair. Every day that a truck is off the road, its owner loses money, which means that an individual with a centre lathe can command high fees for reskimming a scored brake-drum or for rethreading an axle shaft. The average Suame lathe owner, therefore, has none of the discipline required of the manufacturer: the market is readily available; there are no raw materials because the customer supplies the brake-drum or the axle; there is no stock of finished products because there is no product; and there is not even a serious labour problem, as apprentices will actually pay fees for the privilege of working in the shop.

What TCC promotes is very different, requiring individuals who can meet production targets, achieve high levels of machine productivity, produce to exacting standards and tolerances. In return, the service that TCC offers is very special. Training, as well as product development and testing, is the first stage. Access to machine tools—at cost—is a possibility. TCC may sub-contract orders to a client once the business has been established, until markets can be developed. It may assist a client in preparing cash-flow projections for bank loan applications. On rare occasions it may provide equipment on a hire-purchase arrangement. TCC may assist with bulk purchases of raw materials for several small clients, thus reducing production costs. It may be a source of special tools—thread-cutting dies and taps, lathe tools, milling cutters—or, for shops without their own capacity, it may provide a tool resharpening service. TCC engineers are always available for consultations, and TCC will even rent its own equipment on an hourly, daily or monthly basis in order to supplement a client's own workshop capacity.

New truths

'New truths begin as heresies', Huxley wrote, 'and end as superstitions'. If some of the standard criteria for appropriate technology are viewed by TCC as ageing truths bordering on superstition, some of TCC's divergence from the check-list may appear to verge on the heretical. As has been noted, on the light industrial side, from which most of TCC's operations emerge, the entrepreneur is the vehicle, and profit is the engine of technology transfer. While TCC would agree with criteria

61

which stress flexibility, and with technologies that are understandable to and controlled by the user, there are perhaps two other areas of contention with the check-list. The first is the emphasis on renewable energy sources—wind and water power, solar energy, methane gas and pedal power.

In some cases, well known technologies that rely on wind, animal and human power are mature and highly developed, while others are not. As Stephen Salter has pointed out,[7] the bicycle could not have been developed to its present level of sophistication without ball bearings, sprockets, roller chains, free-wheel and gear-changing mechanisms, thin walled drawn-steel tubing and advanced rubber technology for pneumatic tyres. The bicycle is, in fact, a highly complex solution to a common transportation problem. Solar water heaters, windmills and biogas plants, however, with which the appropriate technology movement is so often identified, have yet to reach the levels of simplicity, reliability and cost-effectiveness required to make them acceptable on a widespread basis in most Third World countries.

TCC conducted various experiments in alternative energy sources after the 1973 oil crisis, and some of these will be described in subsequent chapters. But the inevitable solar water heaters that were developed at TCC in the 1970s in most cases lie dormant, silent testimony to shortcomings in cost and reliability, and to the fact that in Kumasi, as in much of Africa, there is cloud cover for 55 per cent of the year's daylight hours. They are both reminders and warnings against what M.K. Garg, the great Indian appropriate technologist, called 'ad hoc improvisations': technologies which are location and person-specific, which may work in one place at one time, but which, regardless of merit, are not universally or even selectively transferable.

Job creation

A final area of conflict with the standard list of AT criteria is the requirement that appropriate technology should emphasize job creation. TCC has not stressed the job creation factor, although as has been noted; it is small-scale industry in Ghana which has produced the most jobs per unit of capital invested, and this is undoubtedly true of enterprises resulting from the TCC experience. The labour problem in Ghana is unusual, however. One of the most dramatic effects of Ghana's straitened economic circumstances was the high rate of emigration among the skilled and semi-skilled work-force, and the 1983 and 1985 expulsions from Nigeria. The figures on the first expulsion, even with significant margin for error, are shocking, and run to hundreds of thousands of people: the highest estimate represents more than 8 per cent *of the country's total population*, and probably as much as 30 per cent of the productive labour-force.

As in many other Third World countries, there are large numbers of unemployed young people in Ghana's urban centres, many of them what Ghanaians call 'disco-minded' youth, the 'Standard VII Boys' and 'Verandah Boys' of earlier days, whose expectations of well paid, comfortable white-collar employment would probably never be fulfilled. In 1981, UST commissioned a survey of farmers within a 25-mile radius of Kumasi, and discovered that less than 10 per cent were under 30 years of age, while 20 per cent were over 60.[8] The economic conditions, the lure of Nigeria, and the all-consuming need to find additional sources of income undoubtedly contributed to Ghana's low labour productivity, which came to be characterized by high rates of turnover and absenteeism.

Examples abound of small industrial and agro-based operations that have attempted labour-intensive technologies and then abandoned them in favour of more capital-intensive approaches. A small palm-oil mill at Dompose, an hour's drive from Kumasi, ordered three of TCC's hand-operated oil presses several years ago. After a year or so of production, however, the owner abandoned them in favour of sending his palm kernels to an automated, government-owned plant several miles away, despite the fact that the automatic mill charged 3,000 cedis per drum of oil, and his own labour-intensive presses could ostensibly do the same work for 1,000 cedis. There were two complaints. The first was that the hand presses were too slow and created a production bottle-neck during which some of his produce rotted, or at least would be unacceptable for human consumption. If he were to increase the number of presses, he would have to hire more labourers, which would not only increase the cost, putting it close to that of the automatic mill, but it would vastly magnify the problem of finding and keeping labour, which in that area was in short supply and highly unreliable—regardless of wages. In the end, it was cheaper and easier for an operation of that size, in that village, to use the apparently more expensive automatic mill. Six miles from Dompose, however, another mill finds local crushing both possible and economical because of different management and labour attitudes, and because of a more effective ratio of equipment to farm size.

Ultimately, the real test in job creation lies not so much in the immediate employment following the transfer of a technology, but in the multiplier effect. A loom may employ a single artisan, but it also creates work for spinners, tailors and retailers. A workshop may employ half a dozen people, but the corn mills it produces may employ hundreds. The TCC approach to job creation and technology is thus tempered by local experience. Appropriate technology in Ghana must provide employment opportunities which fit with the level of skills, the level of interest, and the level of remunerative expectation of the available labour-force. Given the state of the economy and the demand pull from neighbouring countries, the first two criteria in Ghana are perhaps lower than elsewhere, and the third, higher.

CHAPTER 6

Partners in Development

The reluctant partner

It may not be entirely fair to describe the University of Science and Technology as a 'reluctant' partner in TCC's development. At an official level, there has always been a great deal of university support for TCC and its work, and it is obvious from the description of TCC's projects that many faculties took an active hand in the evolution of various important activities. But from the beginning, when some professors saw TCC as an income-generating adjunct to other activities, there was always a degree of tension and misunderstanding. Part of the problem was intellectual: many Third World universities were founded in the shadow of European affiliates, most pursue academic programmes based on international standards and on perceptions relating more to the international than to the domestic academic community.

Most Third World universities would be the first to accept this description. They understandably posit themselves as centres of excellence, critically important in countries only recently exposed to a tradition of western intellectualism and the attendant technological development. If the Third World is to compete successfully and play a meaningful role in the international economy, universities must be on the cutting edge of this development, advancing the frontiers of knowledge; standards of international acceptability must be maintained or surpassed. On the question of technology, many Third World academics are suspicious of the AT movement, seeing it as a proponent of outdated, inferior technology, a form of neo-colonialism intended, either by design or otherwise, to confirm and perpetuate the second rate, dependent position of Third World countries.

The counterpoint to this view, fashionable among development writers, is equally clichéd: Third World universities
have become ivory towers, separated and alienated from the
societies they were established to serve; expensive, elitist
ghettoes which, in shallow attempts to mimic their European
and American counterparts, have squandered precious national
resources. They are neither centres of excellence, nor have they
advanced the cutting edge of development. They produce
theoreticians unable to apply knowledge, they inculcate
selfish, elitist values in their students and they perpetuate
irrelevant curricula, while failing to develop academic and
research programmes aimed at the needs of the community
which pays their keep.

There are unfair distortions as well as elements of truth in
both positions, and variations on either theme can be heard at
the University of Science and Technology. Added to the
intellectual argument is an unspoken emotional one. As a semi-
autonomous body within the university, TCC has all the
advantages of a fully-fledged faculty, with few of the constraints.
It has its own Management Committee, and can negotiate
independent funding from external organizations. Because
foreign agencies are much more eager to fund appropriate
technology than the more prosaic but vitally important
academic programmes of a university, the former tends to be
financially secure, while the latter are increasingly strapped for
funds. A minor technological breakthrough at TCC, regardless
of the state of its advancement, may receive banner headlines in
the local press, but there are few accolades for the professor
who genuinely excites and challenges students with words and
chalk. In short, there is a current of understandable envy
between the university and TCC which has occasionally
complicated the Centre's evolution.

Nevertheless, the administrative and institutional structure
of TCC has remained virtually unchanged since its inception, a
testimony to the wisdom of successive university adminis-
trations. The most important structural aspect is undoubtedly
the early status and autonomy that were conferred on TCC.
Because it is both equal to and separate from the other
faculties, it can work on an equal footing with any one of them.

Its budget is independent of individual faculty interests, and its Director can move freely both within the university and among outside organizations and government bodies. Yet because the deans of all faculties sit on the TCC Management Committee, each has input into policy and programmes, and each is kept regularly informed of what the Centre is doing.

By 1980, a more or less regular income pattern had been established at TCC. That year, 22 per cent of total income was provided in the form of a university subvention allocated from the government's grant to UST. Four per cent was derived from local grants, half in government contributions for special projects; 8 per cent from consultancy fees; 25 per cent from international development organizations and 41 per cent from the earnings of various production units. At about that time, the possibility arose of receiving direct subventions from the government, rather than through the university. The prospect of direct funding had certain obvious attractions, but was also something of a double edged sword. If the subvention came directly from government, its size could be determined on the basis of TCC's relevance to the development and transfer of technology rather than to higher education, with which it was not directly concerned. Conversely, however, increased allocations for higher education would no longer be channelled to TCC. On the other hand, increased government involvement could, in the best of all possible worlds, mean better official understanding and greater overall support, despite the likelihood that, 250 kilometres away in Accra, the government would never completely fathom the campus arrangements which had allowed TCC to flourish.

It was finally decided in 1983 that TCC would receive its subvention directly from the government, but little else changed. The fundamental tie, regardless of income source, was still the University of Science and Technology. TCC still enjoyed office and workshop facilities on the campus despite the successful establishment of two Intermediate Technology Transfer Units. Its senior staff enjoyed the security and perquisites of university appointments, and although TCC enjoyed a degree of management and financial autonomy, its policy was still determined by the University Management

Committee, and its books were still subject to external and university audit.

Ultimately, the real value in the university connection is not the income that TCC might save, or derive from, or even provide to the university; it is in the bridges it can build between the campus and the community. The projects are an important part of this, for TCC is a part of the university and each client knows it. At this level, TCC can take pride in its successes. A bridge connects two places, however, and traffic usually moves in two directions. TCC provides research and on-the-job training opportunities for UST students; it conducts workshops and seminars on various aspects of projects and appropriate technologies. But TCC has had significantly less success in communicating the community to the campus than it has in making the campus useful to the community. Part of this can be ascribed to a defensive campus posture and to the old concerns about 'second-rate technology' in a 'centre of excellence'. This argument will never completely disappear, nor should it, for it carries with it the dynamic tension that is necessary to ensure that 'appropriate' and 'excellence' are synonymous, and that Ghanaian solutions to Ghanaian problems are judged on the quality of their results rather than on preconceived notions about the technologies achieved to reach them.

The silent partner

The relationship between government and TCC is both complex and simple. On a day-to-day level, government impinges on all facets of economic life, and frequent TCC staff trips to Accra are required for the discussion of proposals, and for a myriad of approvals, permissions and explanations. At another level, and taken as a whole, the relationship between the government and TCC has been remarkably constant, cordial and mutually supportive over the years, with government acting not unlike the 'silent partner' of the business world—one whose financial input is essential, but who is content to leave daily management to more active colleagues.

Government financial support has been an essential ingredient in the annual budget of the TCC, originally in the form of subventions made through the university, and since 1983, directly to the Centre. The governmment has also been instrumental in requesting and negotiating certain overseas grants on behalf of TCC. While fluctuations in the Centre's overall income reflect both variations in income from the production units and changes in overseas assistance, the government grant is basically what has paid the core costs of the institution. Actuals often fall short of requests, but it is these core costs, amounting to anything between 10 and 25 per cent of annual income, which have allowed other activities to take place, making TCC attractive to external aid agencies which are often reluctant to cover core administrative or 'programme' costs. For the government, the investment in TCC has a similar attraction; over the years the Centre has demonstrated that every cedi of government input has produced at least four additional cedis in external and production income.

On occasion, the government has also assisted with capital grants. In 1973, it provided a third of the funds required to establish the first soap production unit near Kumasi, a project shared equally with the university and Oxfam Quebec. In 1980, an even more important grant was made, the largest TCC ever received from government, to purchase land in Suame Magazine for the first Intermediate Technology Transfer Unit. This grant, the equivalent of more than US$180,000, demonstrated a significant measure of policy support for the ITTU concept and for small-scale industry in general. The government has also played a part in the assistance TCC has offered its clients, through the granting of special import licences. In 1980, for example, a licence of 100,000 cedis was allocated to TCC for equipment and supplies related to soap production, a second of 30,000 cedis for pigments, and a third of 200,000 cedis for engineering equipment and supplies. Some of the allocations were used by TCC in its own production units, but much of the foreign exchange was made available to clients, most of whom were too small to make individual applications. The fact that the government regards TCC as a trustworthy agent for the identification of suitable small-scale industries is a further measure of confidence. There are other dimensions to the relationship with government. Successive regimes have sought TCC's advice on policies and on the establishment of agencies intended to promote small-scale industry. On occasion, a government minister will visit a TCC project site and, impressed with some aspect of what he has seen, will call for proposals to increase or expand the effort. Invariably, this sort of intervention leads to more paper work than action. One undoubtedly well-meaning minister several years ago announced that government would establish 80 rural palm-oil mills similar to one he had seen using TCC equipment. However, the proposal that was requested of TCC and painstakingly prepared, was never even acknowledged. In 1980, the government announced plans to establish nine ITTUs on the model of the first one opened that year by TCC in Suame Magazine, but beyond TCC's second ITTU in Tamale, the plan has not yet been implemented. Similarly, a succession of small enterprise development bodies has been established by government over the years, but few have born fruit.

Chapters 2, 3 and 4 outlined aspects of the economic and political climate which partially accounted for shortcomings in the promotion of appropriate technology and small-scale industry. But there is another dimension as well, one shared by governments in most countries, rich and poor, north and south. A cabinet minister is judged not so much on the long-term developmental impact of policy, but on immediate results, stated in clear production terms: the number of tons of rice produced in a given period, and the increase or shortfall over the previous year's target. A minister of agriculture will be judged not on what happened to the number of family farms in a year—something which in any case will only be seen in longer-term trends—but on exactly how much grain was produced, usually without reference to long-term impact. A transport minister will be judged on whether produce moves to ports, not on how many small repair shops are damaged by the importation of new trucks rather than the spares which, over a longer period of time, might put more vehicles back on the road at less cost. Production is often stressed at the expense of development because ministers are pressed to make decisions which will yield results in the shortest possible time. Development and production are not mutually exclusive; together they represent what TCC itself aims at, but at a national level where there are different demands and pressures, choices are more difficult, and invariably Third World governments are judged by their own people and by external lending agencies on short-term performance, and on hard figures.

And, too, there are economies of scale in government decision making, as in industry. While TCC can effectively represent 20 or 30 small clients in an application to government for an import licence, and government can be reasonably sure that the funds will be well spent, there are thousands of other applicants in a year about whom government will have only sketchy information. The larger clients, both State Enterprises and those in the private sector, inevitably continue to receive the attention they have always commanded, and regardless of its efficiency or its contribution to the economy, small-scale industry once again takes a back seat. The same is true in agriculture. In 1975, for example, less than 5 per cent of all loans made by the Agriculture Development Bank of Ghana were under 500 cedis. At the time, 500 cedis represented a sizeable amount to the average farmer, certainly more than the cost of a plough, an indication that the government's lending mechanism had been slanted almost exclusively to the large farmer, despite the fact that 90 per cent of Ghana's food was produced by subsistence farmers who owned less than 2.5 acres.

Perhaps the most serious deficiency in government policy over the years, as it relates to small-scale industry, has been the paucity of reliable information on which to predicate decisions. This criticism is equally valid for aid donors. A 1974 World Bank study noted that 'statistical and economic analysts and planners should pay increased attention to conditions and performance in the small-scale sector.' The same phrase appeared verbatim, nine years later, in a 1983 World Bank report, which further noted 'the virtual absence of data on small-scale establishments since 1973.' The absence of such data may reflect a government shortcoming, but it also indicates a lack of donor interest and commitment. The result is that financial allocations may have short-term impact on the symptoms of a problem, but can easily ignore the potential for longer-term solutions. For example, it was estimated in 1983 that 40 per cent of Ghana's heavy goods vehicles were off the road for want of tyres. A World Bank reconstruction credit of US$13.3 million was arranged in order to import enough tyres to put an estimated 3,260 trucks back on the road for eight months. Undoubtedly, the tyres were extremely important to the movement of food and cash crops, for at the time the transport sector was in a state of collapse. Virtually unnoticed, however, and certainly not the subject of any World Bank credits, was the fact that several TCC clients in Suame Magazine were by that time producing thousands of wheel bolts every year from scrap steel and mild steel rod. Tyres or not, a truck with wheel bolts sheared off on a bad road will not move again until new bolts are produced.

Undoubtedly, the positive relationship between TCC and the Government of Ghana will continue, and if policy changes instituted since 1983 are sustained, they may assist the small-scale producer in both the light industrial sector and in rural areas. Much has yet to be done, however. The long-range effectiveness of any policy will ultimately depend on the quality of information available, and on the political will which can be brought to bear by government and donors alike on longer-term development policies as opposed to those aimed at improving statistics in the short run.

Dance partners

Without the support of several international non-governmental organizations, TCC might never have achieved the inertia required to overcome the many obstacles that it faced in its early years. Scottish War on Want, Oxfam, Oxfam Quebec, ITDG and others provided critical financial and moral support at a time when 'appropriate technology' was still somewhat theoretical in its development impact, and when many aid agencies had become disenchanted with institutions of higher learning. The considerable risks they took in supporting TCC are a reminder of the important entrepreneurial role that NGOs play in development work.

By 1975, however, TCC's plans had outstripped the ability of most NGOs to assist with more than specific, small-scale projects. The plan for an Intermediate Technology Transfer Unit in Suame, and another, 400 kilometres north in Tamale, required resources far beyond those available to most voluntary agencies. By fortunate coincidence, at about this time the idea of appropriate technology as a development vehicle had started to work its way into the thinking of several bilateral and multilateral agencies. In November 1975, the government asked the United Nations Development Programme to undertake a study and recommend courses of action that would hasten the growth and improve the productivity of small-scale industry in Ghana. UNDP in turn asked the World Bank if it would execute the study, and the following year, American consultants from Checchi and Company arrived. The Checchi study,[1] submitted late in 1976, remains one of the few authoritative sources of data on small-scale industry in Ghana, and it laid the groundwork for several subsequent reports written by other agencies and consultants. Basically, Checchi recommended a three-year plan to the World Bank entailing an expenditure of US$16 million, improving government focus on small-scale industries and providing significant additional funding for institutions such as TCC. Despite all the activity, however, neither the World Bank nor UNDP accepted the Checchi plan, or for that matter, any other regarding appropriate technology in Ghana.

In the meantime, however, the government, supportive of the ITTU concept and wary of the slow UNDP response, asked the Canadian International Development Agency to assist with the establishment of ITTUs in Kumasi, Bolgatanga and Takoradi, and the upgrading of an existing facility in Tema. That was in July 1976. By May 1977, CIDA's own consultants had visited Ghana and issued a report which, relying heavily on the Checchi findings, 'proposed' that CIDA support the establishment of ITTUs at Tema and Navrongo, and that it accept and support the TCC plan for an ITTU in Suame Magazine. The goal of the proposed project was 'to support the growth of small industries, particularly very small informal enterprises . . . and to contribute to the pool of knowledge on technology transfer so that the Government of Ghana can develop a comprehensive national programme to stimulate the growth of small industries.'[2] Files accumulated as the idea for the project advanced; files, file drawers, filing cabinets full of letters, memos, telegrams, minutes of meetings and professional comments on professional comments. Finally, in April 1979, CIDA gained internal agency approval for a project that had been whittled out of the 1977 proposal: a two-pronged approach to appropriate technology which would include technical assistance (a Canadian adviser) within government to focus on improved policy for small-scale industry, and support for the plan proposed by TCC four years earlier—to establish the ITTU in Suame Magazine. The CIDA assistance amounted to US$210,000, roughly half of which was salaries and support for the technical assistance component at TCC, the balance for equipment and vehicles.

The actual agreement between CIDA and the Government of Ghana was not signed until August 1980, five years after TCC had put forward the plan, and four years after the government's first request to CIDA. CIDA had found the resources in 1979, however, to hire Kevin Davis, a former Canadian University Service Overseas volunteer in Ghana, to assist with the establishment in Suame, and when the government released 500,000 cedis for the purchase of land and construction the following year, the ITTU had at last become a reality.

Almost before the ink was dry on the formal agreement that was signed in 1980, TCC requested that CIDA consider extending the project, realizing now that this could require at least as many months as remained in the original two-year plan. An evaluation was therefore commissioned by CIDA in March 1981, shortly before Kevin Davis was to complete his contract. Davis was prepared to extend for a third year, which would have proven invaluable during the start-up period at Suame, for he was an effective engineer and had quickly developed an easy rapport with clients. An excellent teacher and an artful facilitator, he enjoyed his work and the respect of colleagues and clients alike. The evaluation was fulsome in its praise of the ITTU and of CIDA's contribution in the form of Kevin Davis. The vehicles had proven invaluable, and it was possible to go into considerable detail about the achievements that had been realized since the move off the campus. The report pointed out, however, that 'the "logical framework" for the project, as written by CIDA, assumes a completely programmed series of activities, while the actuality reflects natural growth character-istics.' The report went on to note that 'The project assumes (CIDA) equipment is delivered and used effectively . . . (how-ever) none of the CIDA plant has yet arrived.'[3]

Although CIDA at last agreed to extend the Davis contract, approval came after he had shipped his possessions back to Canada and had made other commitments. And although TCC understood that CIDA was actively considering a project extension in view of the positive evaluation, little happened. In November 1982, CIDA officials visiting Ghana noted an 'apparent lack of interest on the part of the Ministry of Industries, Science and Technology' (ministry officials had been unavailable for a meeting when the team was in Accra), and it was decided that 'the speed of GOG response does not justify more extensive involvement . . .at this time.'[4]

It is hard to know what a bilateral agency means by words like 'interest' and 'speed', but in TCC's experience of CIDA, it had now taken more than half a decade to spring loose a contribution of US$210,000 for the ITTU, the capital costs of which, more than half a million cedis, had been met entirely by the Government of Ghana, in addition to its annual TCC subvention. Nevertheless, TCC was undaunted by the CIDA termination, largely because it was never informed that CIDA had 'closed' the project. In fact, local CIDA staff in Ghana seemed unaware as well, for discussions continued about further CIDA inputs. Regardless of the termination report, another CIDA team arrived at TCC to discuss a three year 'Phase II' for the project. And by early 1984, so much time had passed that CIDA commissioned yet another detailed study of appropriate technology in Ghana.

By now, however, perhaps embarrassed at the delays, CIDA agreed to supply a second engineer for TCC, and proposed a

75

GOOD HOUSE - KEEPING IS GOOD BUSINESS
DON'T CLEAN YOUR MACHINE WHILE IN MOTION

The main machine shop at the Suame ITTU.

one-year grant to tide TCC over until the new plan—now bruited as a five-year effort—could be prepared. The technical assistance was fortuitous, as it allowed a talented young Peace Corps engineer whose contract had expired, to stay on at Suame for another year. The 1984 study had only emerged in tentative draft form by the middle of 1985, but the 'bridge financing', originally proposed in 1983, was finally transformed into a project document which arrived in Ghana for government approval in May 1985, more than a year after the period it was supposed to cover had elapsed. The machinery and equipment it was to pay for had been ordered months before, and in some cases had even been acquired and assembled by TCC's British suppliers. Meanwhile, TCC patiently awaited the unveiling of 'Phase II'.

Through the decade of association with CIDA, TCC's relations were always positive and cordial. The CIDA support, if not invaluable, was certainly welcomed. TCC is hopeful that the relationship will improve and continue, and discouraging words are seldom heard about CIDA in Kumasi. An observer can hardly escape the conclusion, however, that CIDA's bureaucracy and the interminable delays conspired to reduce the effectiveness of its contribution significantly, to negate opportunities, increase costs, and multiply the burden of paper work and bureaucracy in a country where these are already in abundant supply. But if tripping the light fantastic with CIDA was problematic, keeping up with the lateral arabesque performed by USAID across the dance-floor of appropriate technology was even more so.

The United States Agency for International Development had become interested in appropriate technology at roughly the same time as other bilateral donors. Its own consultants had recommended a plan, to begin in 1978, which included half a million dollars to TCC for the establishment of the Tamale ITTU. Eventually, in 1979, a four-year USAID project, budgeted at US$4.8 million was approved and signed by the Government of Ghana. It was called the DAPIT Project— Development and Application of Intermediate Technology— and through it, USAID intended to promote the transfer of appropriate technology using various government research institutions; to establish a special co-ordinating secretariat within government and, *inter alia*, to construct and equip TCC's second Intermediate Technology Transfer Unit in Tamale.

Construction of the Tamale ITTU building was slated to begin in January 1980, so TCC officers and a UST architect hurried north to put the finishing touches on the original 1975 plan. Land was obtained from the City Council in an industrial park, and design of the building was finalized. Then the problems began. USAID felt that shortages of cement and steel in Ghana would seriously retard construction, and decided that a pre-fabricated building, manufactured in the USA, would be faster and cheaper than local construction. This entailed completely redesigning the building, and lengthy delays ensued while complicated US government tendering procedures were observed. The building, which was supposed to have been started in January 1980, was not actually ordered in the US until August 1982, and did not arrive in Ghana until a full year after that. There were further delays while TCC documented for USAID the tendering requirements for local construction of the foundation, and again while a USAID lawyer, flown in from Abidjan, satisfied herself that TCC had correctly obtained title to the land.

Although TCC would have preferred Land Rovers, only $25,000 was available for untied 'offshore purchases' which would have meant receiving only one. USAID offered as an alternative, three Chevrolet diesel pick-up trucks, and so the Centre agreed to the American vehicles. When the trucks arrived in 1982, however, it turned out that petrol engines had been supplied rather than diesel. At a time when virtually no petrol had been available in Ghana for months, this was an impossible handicap for vehicles intended as a lifeline to the north, and to the dismay of USAID, TCC refused acceptance. Finally, a year later, diesel trucks arrived. They were not much better; although spares had been included, the manufacturer had considered only American road conditions. As a result, one of the first things to go, the rubber ends for shock absorbers, were unavailable. There was an electric rather than a manual switch for the second fuel tank which, once broken—as all were within short order—reduced the vehicle's range by half. Dirty fuel and sloshing tanks regularly clogged the fuel line, and to get at the filters, openings had to be cut into the body. Bleeding the unplugged line had to be done with the starter because the 6.8 litre engines could not be hand cranked, and this resulted in dead batteries. Automatic transmissions meant they could not be push started, leading to frequently stranded vehicles and sleepless nights in the bush. To make matters worse, the diesel engines were too heavy for the front suspension, which collapsed with alarming regularity. After two years, at least one of the Chevrolets was always out of action, and the other two were kept on the road only because there was a Peace Corps wizard who had worked on Chevrolets for years in the United States, and a wreck was available that could be cannibalized.

In 1983, at about the time the project was supposed to have been completed, USAID commissioned an evaluation, and hired Checchi and Company, the original AT consultants of years before, to do the job. By the time the Checchi consultants arrived, however, more problems had arisen. A diplomatic incident involving statements made by a government official had resulted in the freezing of all USAID programmes. The Checchi report was devastating. It acknowledged the effects of the economic decline in Ghana and the world-wide recession, but stated unequivocally that 'the design of the project and its administration are at the root of many of the difficulties experienced to date.' Of all the agencies that had been roped into the DAPIT Project, only TCC had proven 'active and energetic . . . using the resources at hand.' The others, basically research bodies that had been persuaded to adopt USAID's objectives as implementing agencies, had not. Much of the equipment for the Tamale ITTU had arrived without connections and accessories required for operation, and in most cases was stored in Kumasi because the prefab building for Tamale had not yet arrived. Essential erection equipment had gone to Lagos instead of Accra. And the freeze meant that individuals hired to work on the project no longer had their USAID salaries. In short, Checchi blamed the failures on faulty project design, an overly ambitious schedule, the national administrative and economic dislocations in Ghana and 'less than energetic project management' by government and by USAID.

When Washington lifted the freeze early in 1984, USAID reacted to the Checchi report with predictable bureaucratic frenzy, demanding that certain 'conditions precedent' be met by the Government of Ghana by June 30; otherwise the project would be terminated. The conditions had been included in the original project design, and government had no doubt been tardy in its observance of them, as had the local USAID administration. But when the conditions were more or less satisfied within the short time-span allotted, USAID cancelled the project anyway, leaving sufficient funds only for the purchase of ancillary equipment left out of the original orders. Appropriate technology was out the window and new projects, with new goals, new objectives and new counterparts had been established.

The Government of Ghana was responsible for some of the delays, but basically, as with CIDA, a bureaucratic behemoth,

1985: The Tamale ITTU nears completion; ten years behind schedule.

encumbered by endless rules, procedures, fears and political interests, had stumbled into the fragile world of small-scale
industry, and in its attempt to help, had vastly inflated costs,
damaged morale, and diverted valuable talent from the business
of development into bureaucratic fire-fighting. The project
agreement, signed in August 1979, resulted in actual completion
of the prefab ITTU building in Tamale *six full years later* in
1985. The foundation work, estimated in 1982—long after it
should have been completed—at 1.7 million cedis, was re-
negotiated in 1983 at 2.6 million cedis, again in 1984 at 6.4
million, and in the end ran to over 8 million cedis.

In the final analysis, TCC got its building in Tamale erected
and equipped, had the services of several talented and
dedicated Canadians and Americans, and for a time enjoyed
transportation facilities that might otherwise have been
unavailable. But it had taken five years to establish the Suame
ITTU, and ten for Tamale, a time factor that would probably
have killed the idea at birth had anyone realized what an effort
it would be. The opportunity cost of servicing donors is always
difficult to estimate, although in TCC's experience of the
bilateral agencies, despite the learning experience, it was very
high.

A possible middle passage between the limited funding capacity of NGO donors and the limited delivery capacity of the bilateral is a mechanism that has become increasingly popular in recent years—bilateral funding *through* NGOs. Rather than attempting to work directly with small development organizations in the Third World, organizations that will never appreciate and may never benefit from bilateral constraints and procedures, some agencies, CIDA and USAID among them, are sub-contracting such work to third-party NGOs. Some of ITDG's support for TCC originated in this way from the British Overseas Development Administration, and although the amounts were smaller than what USAID had envisaged, the money was less tied, was more effectively used, and arrived when it was needed. This is not to suggest that NGOs are uniformly more understanding; TCC has a file with strong letters from Oxfam regarding a Land Rover it had given for Tamale, repeatedly castigating the Centre for not sending the vehicle north, despite the fact that Tamale had been postponed for four years by the USAID mess.

It is not easy to draw constructive conclusions from TCC's experience of the bilateral agencies. It would be simplistic to say that bilateral agencies are incompetent to exert serious positive influence at the grassroots of industry. Such a sweepingly pessimistic conclusion cannot seriously be entertained by most Third World governments for whom aid programmes are an essential part of their development expenditure. And for taxpayers whose contributions finance such organizations, it should be far from acceptable. Nor is it fair to the hard work and commitment that many CIDA and USAID staff put into the projects. In both cases, however, the projects were complicated by consultants who looked at the 'why' and the 'what' of appropriate technology without examining the 'how' of it. It was assumed that if one institution was achieving results, two or three or four times that number could do more with the wave of a project proposal. There was little serious examination of the philosophy, the staff, the structure, the experience, or any of the other things that had contributed to TCC's success in Kumasi.

It may not have mattered, however, for once the consultants' proposals were received, the agencies hammered and hacked and moulded them to suit their own time-consuming procedures for approval and evaluation, their 'logical frameworks' and their tied spending regulations, condemning the projects to senility before they had begun. Fearful of risk, they minimized the discretion of their people in the field and erected road-blocks where there were no problems, yet wasted hundreds of thousands of dollars and jeopardized the very existence of their counterparts, in their interminable delays. TCC's experience of the bilateral agencies confirmed what it had already learned years before: inappropriate procedures will not advance the transfer of appropriate technology.

Working partners

Much development literature focuses primarily on the technical and economic aspects of a problem, often deals gently with the social and political context, and usually ignores the role of individuals completely. Yet the individual players—good, bad, indifferent—the personality clashes, the alliances, the quirks, the affectations, are often critical factors in explaining the success or failure of an endeavour. This is no less true of TCC than of any other institution. The quality of its staff played a key role in the development of the Centre, but perhaps as important was the degree of staff continuity which TCC enjoyed. Clearly the most important individual in the Centre's history was Dr John Powell, who became its first Director in 1972, and who was still piloting the organization at the time this book was completed in 1986.

Powell, a lanky, bearded, almost ascetic mechanical engineer from Dorset, was appointed to the academic staff of UST in 1971 on a four-year contract, and the following year was elevated to the Directorship of the then non-existent TCC. Over the years, one contract led to another; TCC grew; Powell learned to speak fluent Twi; he watched his three young sons mature and eventually return to school and then university in England. A voracious reader, he thought deeply about the role of the university in appropriate technology, and took advantage of his holidays and sabbaticals to study AT institutions in other countries, most notably India. Where others might have seen advantages in independence from the university, Powell steadfastly maintained the importance, especially to the future of Ghana, of relating community development to students. Over the years his writings on appropriate technology, on Ghana and on development have filled volumes; he has been sought out by other Third World universities to advise on the establishment of similar institutions, has delivered numerous thought-provoking and sometimes controversial papers around the world, and at night and early in the morning, he has nursed a lengthy manuscript of memoirs on his experiences with TCC. And yet for all his academic qualifications, publications and philosophical ruminations about appropriate technology, he is essentially a hands-on engineer, happiest when he is actually working on the development of a new project. He travels widely throughout Ghana in a Land Rover which he alone services, always at the wheel himself, paying regular visits to the new ITTU in Tamale, making the rounds of ministries and agencies in Accra, and seeming to be everywhere in Kumasi at the same time.

That he had the intellectual, political and technical skills, as well as the physical stamina to advance the aims and objectives of the Centre over such a long period of time was remarkably fortuitous for the development of appropriate technology in Ghana. And because TCC enjoyed the Director- ship of a single individual over the years, it experienced a continuity that had eluded most similar institutions. This is not to suggest, however, that TCC is the creation of a single person. At all levels of operation the Centre has attracted *and kept* individuals of exceptional talent and dedication. Samuel Arthur, for example, left school when he was a boy and went to work with his brother in Suame Magazine. When the steel bolt production unit was beginning on the UST campus, Arthur was one of the first Suame apprentices brought in for training on machine tools, and 12 year later he was still with TCC, back in Suame at the ITTU where he was now in charge of steel bolt production, with an impressive record of secondments to clients who now produce their own nuts and bolts.

83

Archibald Boateng joined TCC as a production apprentice in 1975 when he was 19, attending night classes at Kumasi Polytechnic. In 1983 he 'graduated', not from the Polytechnic, but from TCC, which assisted him in setting up his own workshop not far from Suame. Today, along with his partners, Boateng successfully produces his own nuts and bolts, and trains his own apprentices. Peter Donkor graduated from the University of Science and Technology in 1972, spent a year teaching secondary school physics and mathematics, and then returned to a job at TCC, where he has been one of the most important technical staff members ever since. Without Donkor, small-scale soapmaking would perhaps have remained a theoretical technology rather than one which has spread widely in Ghana and beyond. He has travelled throughout Africa, establishing soap plants from Guinea-Bissau to Mozambique, and has recently written a book on the subject. Dr Ben Ntim, a member of the original Suame Product Development Group, was Deputy Director between 1974 and 1980, and provided much of the needed continuity at senior levels as well as in the product development field in the Centre's early years. Sosthenes Buatsi, a metal design expert associated with TCC almost from the beginning, and happiest when tinkering with bits of tin, provided the organization and sound management needed to establish and run the Suame ITTU in its first years.

Ghana's National Service Secretariat has supplied TCC with some of its most creative and energetic staff. The Secretariat was established to channel all university graduates into government or development service work, originally for one, then later for two years following graduation. At the outset, many were placed as secondary school teachers to make up for the thousands who had emigrated to Nigeria, but in recent years the organization has focused more on development placements and projects. The first National Service recruit to make an impact at TCC was Kwesi Opoku-Debrah, who gained official appointment after his year of National Service and went on to develop a number of important TCC projects. It was Opoku-Debrah who brought the designs and the impetus for beekeeping back from a trip to Kenya and Tanzania, and who later became so enthused about the prospect of minimum tillage farming that after seven years with TCC, he left to set up his own farm near Kumasi, using the techniques he had been teaching others.

The second National Service appointee was Stephen Adjare, who began as a weaver and then took up beekeeping with such a vengeance that he has established himself as one of Ghana's foremost authorities on the subject. His book *The Golden Insect*[5] has had two printings, and conveys some of the infectious enthusiasm that he applies to all his work with TCC. The third National Service recruit to gain permanent appointment to TCC staff was Peggy Oti-Boateng, originally assigned to act in a liaison capacity for the National Service Secretariat, which in the early 1980s began to request TCC assistance in training its own people in various aspects of appropriate technology. When Peggy Oti-Boateng received her permanent appointment in 1984, she assumed responsibility for ensuring that TCC's projects had the highest possible developmental relevance to Ghanaian women.

Among the Ghanaian staff, there were dozens of others over the years who made valuable contributions to the growth of a consistent philosophy and to the development of an organizational memory. In addition to Ghanaians, notable contributions have also been made by expatriates from a dozen countries in North America, Europe and Asia. Most were on short-term appointments through agencies such as the British Voluntary Service Overseas, the Peace Corps, CIDA or USAID, although there were others in various university departments whose cumulative contribution over a period of years is fondly remembered by staff and clients alike.

Perhaps one of the most colourful individuals to join TCC was Frank Robertson. Robertson, whose youngest child was born in 1985, and who is also a great-grandfather four times over, recalls first seeing a map of Africa in 1929 when he was a schoolboy in Dallas, Texas. The teacher pointed in the general direction of the River Niger and told Robertson, 'that is where we came from.' He never forgot. In 1958, when Kwame Nkrumah visited the USA on a state visit, his speeches about Africa electrified black Americans. In the following years, many went to Ghana; some made it their home, and among

85

them was Frank Robertson, electrical engineer, who would, over the next quarter century, make his own distinctive contribution to development in Ghana. Appointed to co-ordinate USAID's input to TCC's fledgling Tamale operations in 1983, he found himself a year later without a salary when the USAID progrmme was frozen, yet unlike many Americans in Ghana at the time, he stayed and survived on a tiny local allowance. A more unlikely alliance could hardly be imagined than that formed by TCC's academic British Director and the vigorous, street-wise old American in Tamale, but it worked. John Powell ascribes the high calibre of TCC's staff, both the short and long term people, to luck, but Frank Robertson disagrees. 'Doc Powell,' as he refers to the Director, 'knows what he is doing; he doesn't gamble; he doesn't deviate from his objectives. If there are good people at TCC, it is because birds of a feather flock together, and because Doc Powell is taking care of business.'

Clients' Association

Of course, TCC's real working partners are its clients, and they will be more fully described in subsequent chapters. In 1982, however, something happened which demonstrated the high regard in which they held the TCC. Frank Lukey had been a long-time friend of the Centre, as an academic staff member of UST and then, for a year, as Deputy Director of TCC. He was closely involved with many clients, and introduced a number of new projects and ideas over the years. When he was preparing to leave Ghana in 1982, some of the clients organized a farewell lunch for him, and during the gathering, it occurred to them that they should formalize an association, partly in honour of Frank Lukey, but also to further the aims of the TCC and to help each other. Thus was born the TCC Clients' Association, which now has a charter and officers, and holds regular monthly meetings to discuss matters of common concern. Its business is largely practical: the sharing of information on raw materials, government regulations, potential customers. It acts as an unofficial advisory group to TCC, and has occasionally lobbied on its behalf with government. A major aim is to assist newcomers in the business of becoming registered with the Ministry of Industries, in relations with banks, with Customs and Excise, in matters of income tax, incorporation and import licences, all completely baffling to someone establishing a small business. In 1983, the Clients' Association suggested that it work with TCC in mounting a 'Ghana Can Make It' Exhibition in Accra. At a time when the Ghanaian supply of funds, confidence, and even petrol was at an all-time low, the Association contributed 60,000 cedis towards the cost, as well as paying for the entire cost of their own individual booths. It was a remarkable display of solidarity and enterprise, and it provided a necessary morale boost for TCC. Government was favourably impressed, and several of the clients attracted new orders.

In 1985, one of the clients, with the assistance of TCC, was awarded an import licence worth US$50,000, and offered to share the rare and valuable opportunity for imported raw materials with others in the Association. And the Association has long-range plans to reach Ghanaians abroad. Thousands of Ghanaians have emigrated to Europe and North America, intending eventually to return with enough funds for an investment in Ghana. Some who have returned bought machine tools to take with them, but found that they miscalculated their requirements, or misjudged the economic, political or business climate. Many have taken major risks with their savings, and failed. The Clients' Association would like to arrange a pilot workshop, probably in Britain, in order to meet prospective small investors interested in setting up their own productive enterprise in Ghana. They feel that they could paint a realistic picture of risks and opportunities, and could offer constructive advice about the informal sector, of the sort that is rarely available through official channels.

Although it is a small group of individuals, the Clients' Association shows rare public spirit. John Powell explains this admirable quality in terms of the clients' other attributes: they have a capacity for hard work; a willingness to take the calculated risk; the ability to pick themselves up and start over again when things fail. 'We have shown,' he says, 'that although they must start out "selfishly"—acting in their own

87

interest, with the profit motive—they don't go far before looking for ways to assist others. It is a quality they possess because of their other good qualities. When they succeed, they want to help others.'

CHAPTER 7
An Industrial Revolution

In January 1982, John Powell was slated to be interviewed on television in Accra about the work of the Technology Consultancy Centre. The interview, which had been arranged weeks before, took place at a time of great political tension, a matter of days after the Third Republic had been summarily replaced by the Provisional National Defence Council under the Chairmanship of Flight Lieutenant Jerry Rawlings. Rawlings, a charismatic young crusader whose hallmark was clean government, had already held power during a brief anti-corruption sweep in 1979, prior to the re-establishment of civilian rule. The Third Republic ended suddenly on the last night of 1981, and Rawlings took to the airwaves to announce a revolution against corruption and mismanagement. Inflation was running at 300 per cent, increasing the price of a single loaf of bread to more than the official daily wage; the worthless cedi was openly traded on the black market at 15 times its official rate, while Members of Parliament debated wage increases and importation of subsidized automobiles for themselves.

Rawlings called for 'nothing less than a revolution, something that will transform the social and economic order of the country.' Ghanaians should 'take over the destiny of this country, your own destiny, and shape the society along the lines you desire.'[1] People's Defence Committees were established throughout the country to facilitate and protect the social and economic revolution Rawlings talked about, and to fight against the ubiquitous *kalebule*. So when John Powell went on television a few days later to discuss the work of TCC, it was a time of considerable political upheaval, tension and uncertainty, and when the interviewer concluded the discussion by asking Powell if he supported the revolution, there was a moment of complete silence. Foreigners are well advised to avoid domestic politics in any country; despite the temptation, it can prove to be a dangerous minefield from which there are few agreeable exits. Powell looked at the interviewer, thought for a moment, and then replied in his laconic fashion: 'I have always supported a revolution in Ghana,' he said, 'at TCC we call it an industrial revolution.'

The disarming answer was not an idle comment, however, for TCC was deeply involved in a very real industrial revolution in Suame Magazine. For Powell there were four stages of technology: the first and most primitive stage relies on hand tools that are not designed according to scientific principles. The second stage—actually the first stage of development in mechanical terms—involves hand or human powered machines designed in accordance with scientific principles. The third stage relies on scientifically designed machines, powered mechanically and the fourth, not widespread in Ghana, involves the use and development of scientifically designed automatic machinery. In Suame, most workshops had been at stage two when TCC was founded in 1971. A survey of the entire magazine that year uncovered a total of six centre lathes, and almost no other machine tools of any note. A limited survey of only 20 shops in 1984, mostly TCC customers, found 130 machine tools, of which 60 had been provided by TCC. Stage three was well under way. It was an essential development, not only in itself, but because without a local capacity to manufacture plant and machinery, there would be little upward mobility from stages one and two in other sectors of the economy. Ben Adjorlolo's paean to the corn milling machine, the giver of freedom to the ancient Greeks, was not insignificant, for although traditional hand grinding of corn was, by 1975, only a memory in southern Ghana, the simple mechanized corn grinders found throughout the country were almost all imported. Ten years later, however, there was a staggering range of machinery for rural industry and food processing being turned out by TCC clients in Suame and elsewhere.

A partial list includes hoes and cutlasses for the agricultural sector, gate hinges, fence bolts and nuts, planters, bullock carts and ploughs and slasher blades for tractors. For palm-oil extraction there were presses, boiling tanks, palm-fruit pounding machines and kernel crackers. In the woodworking sector there were carpenter's saw benches, wood-turning lathes and small tools such as hammers and chisels, while new products for the woodworking industry included broadlooms, warping mills, and beehives. There were soap-boiling tanks, caustic-soda plants, smokers for beekeepers, charcoal kilns and driers, and pyrolysis plants, and on the food processing side, gari plants, gari presses and corn mills.

The development and use of some of these products will be described in subsequent chapters; however, few of the rural enterprises they supplied or created would have been possible without the light engineering industry fostered by TCC. It was this side of the Centre's work which lay at the heart of its success, which demanded and justified the care, attention and the great amounts of time that were devoted to it. The engineering workshops are, in a sense, the real middlemen of appropriate technology. Spurred by the profit motive, they ultimately handle the thorny questions of finance, labour, politics and productivity that bedevil so many organizations—foreign and local, university, government or voluntary—that attempt to reach the grassroots through the transfer of technology.

SIS Engineering

SIS Engineering began operations in a small shack at Anloga, a swampy carpentry section of Kumasi, in 1972. The original name, 'School Science Import Substitution Enterprises' belied its humble beginnings, but gave a clue to its origins. In 1969, Frank Lukey and two young technicians at the UST Physics Department began to produce small orders of equipment for Ghanaian secondary schools. It started with requests for standard resistance plug boxes which were needed for GCE 'O' level practical examinations, and eventually, as imported equipment became more and more scarce, requests to the UST Physics Department grew. Orders soon outstripped the ability of the Physics Department to cope, and production shifted first to Frank Lukey's garage, and then in 1972 to Anloga. The two technicians, one of whom was Solomon Adjorlolo, had formed a commercial partnership and had obtained two small wood-turning lathes, an electric drill and a universal wood-working machine, with assistance from Scottish War on Want. By now, the workshop was producing a range of equipment—decade resistance boxes, metre slide-wire bridges and jockeys, wooden optical benches, pendulum bobs and other items, and when Solomon Adjorlolo was offered an opportunity to take a course in plant engineering and maintenance in Britain, his younger brother, Ben, resigned from his job and moved to Anloga to manage the workshop.

By 1973, their product range had expanded to 36 items, including drawing boards, tripods, T-squares, ammeters, voltmeters and rulers, and prospects for expansion looked especially promising when Ghana announced that it would soon adopt the metric system. Ghana was headed on its long downward economic slide, however, and the hopeful beginnings of a business in school equipment faded with the evaporation of funds for education. Attempts were made to diversify into toy production and more sophisticated science equipment, but markets for these were fast disappearing as well. Some orders came from TCC, for soap moulds and soap-cutting tables. The shop produced a number of the 40-inch English broadlooms that TCC was developing at the time, but as cotton thread disappeared from the market, so did opportunities for weavers. Through TCC, trial export orders were arranged for wooden tool handles and wall plaque blanks for a Scottish heraldry firm, but the initial orders were not repeated, and the expensive research and development costs that had gone into them were lost.

In an attempt to diversify, SIS purchased a metalworking production lathe in 1974, planning to produce metal jigs and cutters for carpenters, but found it difficult to keep the machine fully occupied. This led to a search for new work, and SIS began to undertake repairs of spindle bearings for local circular-sawbench operators. TCC staff worried about the continuing viability of the company as one market after another dried up in the withering economy; through the mid-1970s, about 30 per cent of the workshop's sales were the result of contracts provided by the Centre. At the time, TCC was still looking for the elusive mechanism by which steel bolt and nut manufacture could be transferred from the campus, and in 1976, when it decided to sell some of its own production equipment to potential producers, SIS Engineering was a prime candidate.

In January 1977, a capstan lathe was transferred from the campus and installed at Anloga in the expectation that SIS Engineering would become the first private manufacturer of nuts and bolts. Production at SIS was slower than on the campus, however. The lathe was used for nuts and bolts for half the available time, and labour productivity at Anloga was about 70 per cent of what it had been on campus, adding up to a rate of productivity which was 35 per cent of potential, or half of what TCC had enjoyed on the campus. Part of the problem was that the mark-up on nuts and bolts was less than that which could be realized on other products, and in the interest of cash flow, nuts and bolts took second place.

At about the same time, because of the repairs SIS had been doing for Anloga sawbench operators, they began to actually

Wood turning lathe developed by SIS Engineering.

93

manufacture spindles and bearing housings for sawbenches, and before long, with the use of a welding set that Solomon Adjorlolo had obtained from Germany, they began fabricating complete sawbenches out of scrap steel. Not long afterwards, they produced their first wood-turning lathe and soon a dozen were in operation. In their modest way, the SIS circular sawbench and wood-turning lathe were to Anloga what the Spinning Jenny had been to the textile industry in 18th-century Britain. Within five years, Anloga was transformed. Once a relatively small cluster of carpenters and sawyers turning out basic wooden furniture and fittings, it now stretched for a kilometre along a muddy stream, a noisy area not unlike a small Suame, where the scream from SIS-made sawbenches reverberated from dawn till dusk.

By 1985, SIS had sold 35 in Kumasi and as many again to other customers throughout Ghana. Some of the sawbenches found their way as 'unofficial exports' to Burkina Faso, Nigeria and the Ivory Coast, where harder currency was used to purchase blades, bearings, tools and motors to feed the growing business in Anloga. Carpenters discovered that the sawbenches could convert offcuts from the many Kumasi sawmills into useful items, and so a new use was discovered for something that had hitherto gone largely to waste. And the wood-turning lathes produced new wooden products—bowls, furniture legs and components that had previously remained in the hands of a few large capital-intensive firms in Accra. Through the efforts of SIS Engineering to find new products and new markets, a whole industrial area had been transformed.

It was not all joy and happiness for SIS, however. The economic decline invariably meant that many customers could not pay, large orders were almost impossible to find, labour turnover was high as trained apprentices departed for Nigeria, and inflation made planning almost impossible because even the scrap used in product manufacture seemed to escalate in price on a daily basis. In addition, basic consumables such as cutting tools and welding rods could not be imported without going through interminable government procedures, entailing delays of as much as a year. The alternative, searching out what was needed on the black market, meant paying extortionate prices. In 1979, SIS paid off its loan for the original capstan lathe purchased from TCC and soon afterwards ceased production of steel bolts, converting the machine into a centre lathe in order to increase production of bearing housings and spindles for the carpenters. At the same time, the Adjorlolo brothers began to take a close look at corn milling machines.

SIS had reached a stage in its development where ideas, techniques and market development were largely within its own capabilities, and TCC assistance was now limited to specific one-off consultancies, a few sub-contracts, and the essential supply of imported consumables and equipment. After some experiments in copying an imported corn milling machine, SIS developed a viable local variant. The imported model had a bronze bushing which wore out quickly and was difficult to replace, so they substituted a ball bearing—widely available both through *kalebule* and from various cannibalized sources—which increased the speed slightly, and therefore the output of the machine. Since mild steel was unavailable for the main shaft, SIS used broken half shafts from trucks, and found that the better steel prolonged the life of the machine. Cast iron technology was unavailable to SIS for the grinding wheels, so the Suame ITTU started to produce cast iron wheels to supply them with an alternative to the imported variety which they had previously been forced to use. Not only was SIS now producing a machine that was all but impossible to obtain in Ghana, it was saving considerable foreign exchange in the process. The first models produced in 1978 were sold for 3,000 cedis, against an official price of 7,000 cedis for the imported model. By 1982, the SIS corn mill was selling for 18,000 cedis while the imported model, available only through smuggling, sold at 50,000 cedis. By 1985, inflation had driven the SIS price to 55,000 cedis, against the imported price of more than 100,000.

In the early 1980s, SIS was assisted by TCC in obtaining further equipment in order to increase and diversify production, which now included corn hullers, kernel crackers, cassava graters and presses and a palm-fruit pounder, as well as sand/soil/cement block presses and other woodworking equip-

95

ment. In order to maximize the use of his machinery and labour, Solomon Adjorlolo would take the occasional repair job, but these were largely reserved for the private income of his workers, of whom there were now more than a dozen. He had hit on the idea of allowing his skilled technicians to use the machines for their own work at lunch-time and in the early evening, and as a result he had stabilized his labour turnover, one of the most severe handicaps for any small business in Ghana, without inflating his prices through a massive wage bill. By taking small orders to drill holes or add bushings to randomly imported saw blades for example, Adjorlolo estimated that in a few hours, workers probably tripled what he paid them. While the net result in the restraint on his own wage bill was actually an increase in his workers' hours, it solved the perennial Ghanaian dilemma of workers' need for discretion and control over a portion of their own time and earnings, and it gave them an income that Adjorlolo could never have paid.

Although credit is no longer a problem for SIS, it certainly was throughout its first difficult decade. The first simple woodworking equipment was obtained through personal loans, but in order to expand, Solomon Adjorlolo approached and was turned down by some of the best: the Management Development and Productivity Institute offered a trader's loan, with a repayment schedule which was to begin the day the loan was signed, despite the fact that the equipment he wanted to order would have taken a year or more to arrive. Standard Bank turned him down, and so did Barclays. Without loans from Scottish War on Want and the British United Reformed Church, and TCC's willingness to sell some of its own equipment, SIS would probably never have lasted more than two or three years. To have awaited official sanction for foreign exchange and import licences at almost any point in the company's history would have proven disastrous, as SIS had been forced to alter its market and production line several times in order to survive the volatile fluctuations in the economy. By 1985, however, SIS had, in a sense, come of age. The Ministry of Industries, Science and Technology granted SIS Engineering an import licence worth US$50,000 for construction materials, on the basis of its performance in the local manufacture of food processing equipment.

Today, SIS Engineering is a going concern. Although it still operates under ramshackle conditions amidst the noise and sawdust of Anloga, the shop has been expanded several times and is now probably one of the best equipped in Kumasi. The Adjorlolo brothers paid for everything they own at prevailing market prices, surviving failures that would have daunted the most intrepid entrepreneur anywhere, and they developed new products which were clearly helping Ghana into the third stage of technology. Because they knew business was coming, they could look ahead; they could plan their income and, unlike many small enterprises in the informal sector, they could pay their taxes. They knew there would be profits, but they also gained obvious satisfaction from their work, and from the stability and long-range security it had given them.

Josbarko Engineering Enterprise

TCC had hoped that SIS Engineering would become the first off-campus producer of steel nuts and bolts when it sold Solomon Adjorlolo one of its own capstan lathes in 1977. Although SIS did produce nuts and bolts for a year or so, the capstan lathe was turned to other uses in 1979 and no further nuts and bolts were made. By that time, TCC had been manufacturing its own nuts and bolts successfully, profitably and *appropriately* for seven years without anyone taking up the example. There were customers aplenty, small ones and larger ones who placed bulk orders retailing the nuts and bolts to secondary customers in other parts of the country. But no producers. One of the larger buyers was a man who had started his working life as a pharmaceutical laboratory technician, leaving his job at Mbrom Hospital in 1975 to become a self-employed trader. Joseph Barima Kwaako, a short, stocky, soft-spoken man of middle age, was perhaps one of the least likely of TCC's hundreds of acquaintances to become a manufacturer of nuts and bolts.

Kwaako's search for business carried him all over southern Ghana and he first arrived at TCC in 1976, having heard about nuts and bolts, and knowing of a potential customer with special requirements. The Kofifoh Boatbuilding Company in Accra was in the business of manufacturing diesel powered, ocean-going fishing boats up to 75 feet in length, and their need for specialized nuts and bolts was running headlong into the shortages caused by the foreign exchange problem, *kalebule*, inflation and government red tape. Joseph Kwaako had the customer; TCC had the product; both had a sale, and soon Kofifoh Boatbuilders were the largest single consumer of TCC nuts and bolts. Because he was handling a considerable volume of bolts, and the cash required to pay for them, Kwaako put two and two together and soon came up with the idea that if TCC was looking for a client to produce nuts and bolts, there was no one more appropriate than himself. At TCC, however, the idea at first seemed preposterous; Joseph Kwaako had few of the attributes on TCC's client profile list. He had no mechanical skills; he had been self-employed only a matter of months; and far from being a producer, he was a trader—the antithesis of what TCC wanted.

But Kwaako persisted. In 1978, he sent his son to TCC as an apprentice. He asked TCC to help him design a workshop, and he had a concrete floor and wooden building constructed to house it on a plot of family land half a mile from Suame. In 1979, he achieved the impossible by having three-phase electricity connected to the building. By now, his drive and determination could not be doubted, for he had given up most of his trading work in order to get 'Josbarko' established. At the time, courtesy of ITDG, TCC had a number of used machine-tools on order, and finally decided that Kwaako should be allocated enough equipment to start his own production unit. At the last moment, however, financing for the machinery became a problem. Although the Social Security Bank, with whom Kwaako had saved for several years, had asked TCC to recommend potential loan candidates, they took one look at the laboratory technician-turned-trader and declined the request to participate in nuts and bolts. Kwaako was now in trouble, having neglected his customers and having invested everything he owned in the land and building for his workshop, and so, against its own better judgement, TCC

98

offered to provide the equipment on a hire-purchase agreement. Kevin Davis, the CIDA man at TCC, and Samuel Arthur, who had joined TCC in its first years, were assigned to Kwaako. Arthur was seconded to the shop for three months, and when the machine tools arrived, Davis set them up and helped start the initial production runs. Before long, the machines—two capstan lathes, a milling machine, a drill and a grinding machine—were running and production was under way.

The equipment was supplemented a short time later by the addition of a welding machine, because a new production technique had been developed in order to save materials. Originally, a bolt had been made entirely from a single piece of mild steel rod, usually 'bending rod' produced from recycled scrap at the Tema Steelworks. First the rod was straightened, and a hexagon bar was produced from it by horizontal milling. The hexagon bar was turned on a lathe, producing a round bolt

Joseph Kwaako (centre) instructs a lathe operator at Josbarko.

99

of the required length, then cut off with a small piece of the remaining hexagon for the head. The thread was applied in a secondary lathe operation, using a radial die head. Nuts were produced from the hexagon bar through which a hole had been drilled and threaded on the drilling machine using a tapping attachment. This was a costly method of producing bolts, however, as a good part of the hexagon bar wound up as shavings on the floor. The new method was more straight-forward. Rod was selected as close to the size of bolt required—1/2 inch, 5/8 inch, 3/4 inch—sending as little to the floor as possible. Thread was then applied to *both* ends, and a nut screwed firmly to the top. The nut became the head and was then welded to the bolt and faced off for neatness. The result was a more efficient product which avoided wasting material, yet still produced a strong bolt.

Kwaako was also provided with tangential die heads for his capstan lathes, a new departure. Until 1979, all TCC bolts had been threaded using radial die heads, which, although they could be reground, had a life expectancy of less than 2,000 bolts, depending on the length of thread produced. A further problem had resulted from the fact that every thread form used in the world (BSW, BSF, UNF, UNC, Metric Coarse, Metric Fine) and at least ten sizes in each were both commonly used and frequently demanded in Suame Magazine. The number of taps and dies required if Josbarko was going to satisfy the demand would be unimaginably high. When presented with the problem, ITDG recommended the tangential die head. Not only could it be reground more often, increasing the life expectancy by eight or ten times, it could be adjusted to produce different threads on bolts of different diameters. It was not only more versatile and durable, it also speeded up production considerably, and by 1980 had become the preferred technology for threading bolts at TCC.

Because Kwaako was known as a trader and not as a manufacturer of nuts and bolts, at the beginning, TCC subcontracted its own orders to him. The irony was that where he had once carried orders from the Kofifoh Boatbuilders to TCC, now TCC was taking orders from Kofifoh and giving them to Kwaako. The tables had been reversed, although this would last only a year until he could establish his own credibility as a producer. By 1981, he was confident enough of himself and the quality of his product to begin to set his own prices, reflecting actual market costs rather than those established in the somewhat artificial setting of TCC. In addition to the obvious entrepreneurial and technical skills that Kwaako either brought to his new vocation or learned along the way, he had a formidable sense of forward planning, as evidenced by an ability to save and to reinvest in his shop, avoiding one of Ghana's most common failings, premature profit taking. 'I don't want to owe,' he said simply, using his slow periods to produce for stock, knowing that customers would always return.

Because Josbarko was the first important manufacturer of nuts and bolts, TCC paid close attention to Kwaako's production figures and finances. The loan was paid off in short order, and he was able to purchase his welding machine and a hacksaw from profits. In 1982 he took a second loan, this time from the Small Business Loan Promotion, and purchased an additional milling machine, another capstan lathe, a centre lathe and a master tool-cutter/grinder. That loan was liquidated within two years, all from the production and sale of nuts and bolts. In 1979, Josbarko produced 20,000 sets of nuts and bolts and the following year increased production by 50 per cent. Kwaako's volume for 1982 and 1983 remained at roughly 20,000, and in 1984 he took on a new product: spark-plug extenders. A plug extender is a steel device screwed into the cylinder head of an engine in order to raise the spark plug half an inch or so from its normal setting. In engines nearing the end of their lives, as so many in Ghana are, a plug extender will cut oil consumption and reduce the incidence of engine failure from dirty plugs. It is a simple idea, and it took Joseph Kwaako about an hour to produce one from a sample given to him by a trader. In 1984 he produced 4,000 of them on order, and the demand showed no signs of abatement.

Joseph Kwaako, like all small-scale producers in Ghana, had his problems. Labour was one of the most serious. His son, carefully trained at TCC, suddenly left one day for Nigeria, as did a series of technicians and apprentices. In his first 18

101

months, despite the competitive wages he paid, he lost five employees out of a total work-force of five. Absenteeism and pilferage, despite his own regular presence in the shop, also worked against productivity. And he complained bitterly about the shortage of raw materials. Tema steel is often of poor quality and if a machine operator is not careful, valuable equipment can be damaged. Even the most common mild steel rod is often not available, and pricing is a constant headache because of inflation. Nevertheless, Josbarko has made money. Unlike so many small-scale entrepreneurs, Joseph Kwaako ploughed all his profits back into the business, paying off his loans and taking new ones to expand his plant and production line. The demand for nuts and bolts will continue, and though there are now other producers as a result of TCC's work and Kwaako's pioneering example, he is not worried about competition. It will only result in a better product and a realistic price, he feels.

A detailed case study of Josbarko Enterprise in 1981 drew five conclusions regarding the road-blocks in front of creative individuals like Joseph Kwaako and SIS Engineering: they face a shortage of raw materials, both local and imported; equipment and consumables are in short supply because they are not locally produced and foreign exchange for importation is non-existent; credit facilities do not favour the small entrepreneur; skilled labour is in short supply and most labour, skilled or unskilled is low in productivity for both social and economic reasons. That notwithstanding, Kwaako had established an important precedent.

At TCC, people speak highly of Joseph Kwaako, not only because of what he has accomplished, but because of the unlikely background from which he emerged. 'While this country abounds with skilful traders who are adept at taking a fast profit in almost any economic climate, those who are far-sighted enough to build a productive enterprise of lasting strength are few and far between,' wrote John Powell in 1981. 'In a decade of small industry development projects, TCC has encountered less than a handful of such men. [Joseph Kwaako] is one of them.'[2] Kwaako is quick to praise TCC for the large part it played in his success, and his gratitude is eloquently and simply expressed in the names he has painted on his first two capstan lathes: one is named 'Dr Powell', and the other, 'K. Davis'.

Men for all seasons

Archibald Boateng joined TCC as an apprentice at the age of 19 and learned how to make nuts and bolts from the bottom rung of the ladder. He watched Joseph Kwaako's progress and listened to him whenever he came to the production unit. Gradually, he developed the idea that he, too, could go into production for himself. By 1981, Kwaako was established, and Boateng, now 25, decided to take the plunge. It was two more years before the idea came to fruition; he had to organize a partnership with two friends, and arranging a shop was more difficult than he had imagined, but in 1983 BOD Enterprises opened its doors and produced its first spring centre bolts.

Gilbert Workey had done the same four years earlier. He started at TCC as a senior technician in 1973 and began thinking about his own shop three or four years later. It took him until 1979 to organize the funds and the location, but when the first used machine tools for TCC arrived from Britain in 1979, he was ready and waiting. His 'Workshop of General Technology' which today employs four young men, developed a mixed production—some nuts and bolts and some plant construction, often ordered through TCC: water tanks, soap-boiling tanks, palm-kernel crackers and pepper grinders.

Gamatco Engineering began production in 1982, operating with four or five men from a shop rented at the back of the Suame ITTU, with used machine tools imported on their behalf by TCC. They specialized in gears and sprockets, for which there was great demand. The gears were all produced from scrap steel, as iron castings were unknown in Suame, and the sprockets were cut from old boiler plate. Raw material did not present Gamatco with an insurmountable problem, for if they could not find what they wanted in Suame, they ranged farther afield to the gold mines and the large sawmills which were among their customers. One of their most important customers was the Tomos Motorcycle Factory in Kumasi,

*Scrap steel at Gamatco Engineering
from which sprockets will be made.*

Finished sprockets produced from scrap at Gamatco Engineering.

which assembled imported components for a Yugoslavian motorcycle. As with all firms in Ghana, Tomos was starved of the foreign exchange required to produce, so any import substitution possibility was eagerly exploited. Gamatco had been successfully producing small lots of front and rear sprockets for a variety of Suzuki and Honda models, and so their offer to fill bulk orders for Tomos was eagerly accepted. In 1985, Gamatco was turning out as many as 200 pairs of sprockets a month. While their price ran anywhere from 50 per cent to 100 per cent more than the imported version, the foreign exchange component was minimal, and their price disadvantage dropped steadily as the exchange rate of the cedi shifted in favour of local production.

For Gamatco, as for others in Suame, one of the biggest problems over the past few years has been the supply of electricity. The drought of 1982–3 severely lowered the water level behind the massive Akosombo Dam, and the first priorities for rationed hydro-electric power were large manufacturing establishments in Accra, and then exports of electricity to Togo in return for foreign exchange. In the early 1980s, the power was off as much as half the day in Suame, and occasionally for days at a stretch, costing small production units like Gamatco dearly. Rationing was not the only problem, however. Suame Magazine was badly overloaded, and the only solution, apparently, was to lay a new underground cable for half a kilometre into the Magazine. Using $15,000 of CIDA funds, TCC arranged to have the cable laid, but a shortage first of connectors and then of the traditional 'connection fee' delayed a reliable source of electricity for more than two years after actual installation of the cable.

Frank Awuah is a 'self-made' man. With his only qualification a primary school education, he joined a large foreign-car dealer as an apprentice mechanic, and in 1960 decided to go abroad to further his education and earn enough money to make an investment in his future. Travel, immigration and work permits were easier in those years than they are today, and it was possible for Frank Awuah to purchase a ticket to Britain for £60, and to land with less than £20 to his name. He began by working in the motor vehicle section of a dairy in Leeds, while

105

studying at night. Later, he moved to London and worked for British Railways as a motor fitter, then at a workshop in Brixton. In all, he worked and saved for 14 years in Britain, taking night classes and correspondence courses in plant and production engineering for more than half that time. In 1974, he arranged an appointment with a British firm operating in Ghana, and returned home, eventually putting the equipment for which he had saved so long into operation in 1978.

The shop he established concentrated on engine reboring, but after a couple of years he realized that he did not have enough equipment to make the shop pay for itself. He had resolved to return overseas for a few more years to earn enough for what he needed, when he heard about TCC. The large centre lathe that he wanted now became a short-run possibility for Frank Awuah. Few things in Ghana seem to move quickly, however; although he had been dealing with the Ghana Commercial Bank for seven years, they were reluctant to lend him the 28,000 cedis he needed. Finally, with TCC backing, he secured the loan and in 1982 the machine arrived. Eight feet in length, it was the biggest lathe TCC had imported, far too large for Awuah's little shop, so, like Gamatco, he rented premises from TCC behind the Suame ITTU. The first machine was followed in 1983 by a milling machine, a tool grinder and a second welding machine.

Awuah's first output was valve seats on cylinder heads but soon, using the TCC method, he moved into production of wheel bolts for heavy goods vehicles—Albion trucks, Mercedes, Bedfords and others. Because of the high quality steel required, he produced most of his wheel bolts from broken axle shafts he picked up around the Magazine. The shortage of wheel bolts in Ghana is a chronic and heavy drain on the productivity of the transport sector, and therefore on the economy as a whole. Drivers have a tendency to over-tighten bolts which, combined with the terrible road conditions, makes them early candidates for destruction. Concentrating only on wheel bolts and nuts, Frank Awuah can produce more than a thousand a month, but he prefers to mix his production, both to use his equipment more efficiently, and to vary his mix of customers and income.

In 1983, for example, he began to produce piston rings for

small engines. But his most interesting product was a simple item he invented himself in 1982. He owned a small Volkswagen which was on its last legs, burning excessive amounts of fuel and raising the level of noise pollution in Suame with its knock. The problem was well enough known to Volkswagen mechanics; the weight of the flywheel wears the front of the crank-case, until eventually the knock and oil leakage demand a replacement. In 1982, however, a Brazilian-made crank-case cost 24,000 cedis, which meant that most Volkswagens, including Frank Awuah's, were headed for oblivion. Undaunted, he took the engine apart and studied the problem. First he straightened the crank-shaft. Then he made a special fixture to hold the crank-case on his big lathe, and he enlarged the crank-shaft opening. He produced a precision bearing of aluminium, put the engine back together and started it up. It worked. He drove the car for a month without problem, then two months, then six before deciding that he had a product. Since then, he has put nearly a hundred Volkswagens back on the road at a cost of less than 3,000 cedis each, a saving for the customer, one-tenth the cost of the imported crank-case, and a significant saving in foreign exchange.

New clients

There really is no such thing as a 'new' client at TCC, because it may take several months of contact before an individual is actually considered a client, and by then, a solid relationship has developed. Nana Edward Abrefah became involved with TCC in 1982, yet by mid 1985, he had not actually received any hardware through the Centre. Abrefah had worked for years as steward for a British missionary who returned to England permanently in 1976. He then decided to go into business for himself, opening a tiny panel-beating shop in Suame where, after a couple of years, he joined forces with a Nigerian blacksmith. When the Nigerian left for home, Abrefah bought his equipment, and in 1982 he approached TCC about the possibility of getting machinery.

The first step was to decide exactly what he needed, and then to train him to operate similar machines at the ITTU. In 1985,

107

his product line extended to more than fifty items—handles and levers, 'washermen's pressing iron', parts for door locks, slasher blades for tractors, chisels and various hammers—chipping hammers, stone-breaking hammers, claw hammers, sledgehammers. Abrefah employed three people, and worked with an anvil, a vice, a small forge he made himself, and a variety of hand tools. Access to the ITTU equipment, however, which he rented at 50 cedis an hour and now operated entirely himself, broadened his production line, improved its quality and increased his capacity. He could point with pride to a hammer of the sort he sold in bulk to a large Accra department store following the 'Ghana Can Make It' Exhibition, which he attended with the TCC Clients' Association. That order, for 120 hammers, was worth 40,000 cedis, and when his new machinery arrives, he will be able to take on much more production of his own. The equipment—a shaper, a centre lathe, a welder and a drill—await only the elusive signature on the long delayed 'Phase II' of the CIDA project, first mooted before Edward Abrefah had actually heard of TCC.

Kwame Appiah was another client who was eager for the CIDA project to be approved, but for him the delay was more serious. Appiah studied at the Sunyani Technical Institute and was working at the UST Department of Mechanical Engineering when he heard about TCC. He had always hoped that some day he might have a workshop of his own, and his aged father was willing to assist with the finances. But time was of the essence, because in Ashanti, children do not inherit from their father. When a man dies, his wealth goes to his nephew. Appiah's father had therefore to assist his son in this life, and in 1983 he deposited 100,000 cedis with TCC against the order of machine tools awaiting CIDA approval. Then Kwame Appiah went to work at TCC to learn the trade, first in the nut and bolt section, and after a year in the plant construction unit making soap-boiling tanks, rotary punch-planters and palm-fruit boiling tanks. His younger brother also joined TCC as an unpaid apprentice so he would be able to assist when the equipment arrived. As the months stretched out, Appiah had his shop constructed in Suame, including a solid concrete floor, and even managed to have the electricity hooked up.

When the CIDA Phase II goes ahead, Appiah will probably have worked at TCC for more than three years waiting for his equipment. In itself, this is not a major problem, for he will have become well versed in his chosen field by the time he is ready to start production. The problem is that the 100,000 cedis he deposited in 1983 against specific machine tools was worth more than US$36,000 at the prevailing exchange rate. With the 1984 devaluation, its value dropped to US$3,300, then in 1985 it fell to $2,000 and then $1,886. TCC hoped to be able to salvage some of the elder Appiah's life savings by negotiating a shadow rate of exchange for orders placed before the devaluation, but much depended on CIDA and the length of time it would take to get the project, planned for 1983, under way.

Kwame Appiah's problem raised a question: with such dramatic rates of devaluation, how could the small entrepreneur afford machine tools which had suddenly jumped 20 times in cost? Although the answer would not help Appiah, who was caught between rates, the effects of the devaluation would have limited effect because inflation, while not as high as it once was, would smoothe off some of the devaluation's sharp corners, and because the new cost of equipment would ultimately be reflected in the selling price of goods produced by the machinery. Although scientific costing is rarely done in Suame, the addition of a lathe at 20 times the previous price to a shop with three machine tools, using 20 per cent as the rate of depreciation, might add 5 per cent to the cost of production. Obviously it would be higher for an entirely new enterprise, but in actual fact, the concept of depreciation is virtually unknown in Ghana; machine tools actually appreciate in value, the more so with devaluation. Ultimately, however, even if a finished bolt or a corn mill increases in price because of the devaluation, the simple fact is that it will never increase through devaluation alone by as much as the imported product it is replacing. If anything, devaluation was most likely to help, rather than hinder, small-scale import-substitution enterprises.

Anthony Owusu-Amankwatia is a recent acquaintance of TCC. He returned to Ghana in 1983 after six years working in Britain as an electrical technician. He had invested all his savings in a large 13-foot centre lathe, a drill, a grinding machine and a power hacksaw, and brought them back to Ghana with him. Although electricity was his field, he knew he would never lose his capital if he put it into machine tools, and in any case, he had unbounded enthusiasm and the determination needed to make them pay their way. His first disaster was obtaining land. He was able to get a plot only on the northern edge of Suame, bordering fields and the forest beyond, a place far from the nearest electricity. So he invested in an expensive locally made generator, but within days it had cracked through poor alignment. Friends suggested he contact the ITTU where Ralph Moshage, a former Peace Corps volunteer now on a CIDA contract, was acting manager. Moshage repaired and aligned the generator and helped set up the centre lathe, and in talking with Amankwatia, began to see the potential for a longer relationship.

By mid-1985, the direction it would take was still uncertain. Amankwatia was plagued by the enormous cost of running his generator, and knew that he needed more equipment and greater production to justify the expense. He was taking repair work in order to keep everyone working, machining condemned cylinder linings to fit slightly smaller engines: Toyota to Ford 5000 tractors, 'Benz' to Albion, MAN diesel to '1621', and so on. But he was dissatisfied with the erratic nature of repair work, seeing longer term security in production. He sent some of his people to the ITTU to learn how to make a palm-oil press, and was subsequently given a TCC order for ten, which he completed successfully and quickly. He was also given work manufacturing bushings and fittings for bore-hole pipes in connection with a TCC water project, and these, too, were successful. Possibly the relationship will mature, for Amankwatia has demonstrated the drive and determination TCC seeks. It could mean more orders; possibly TCC could help with toolings and other accessories, but as with all clients, the evaluation process was a mutual exercise which would only ripen with time.

Job creation, used machine tools and other philosophical questions

Having described in greater detail some of the TCC clients, the environment in which they work and the products they produce, it is now possible to return to some of the philosophical matters addressed in Chapter 5. The first is the question of the profit motive. It can be seen from the examples provided that TCC's clients are small, so small that most are officially categorized as 'micro-industries' rather than 'small scale'. While there are clearly sufficient profits to pay off loans and keep workshops in business, there are few overnight fortunes being made, and the sector is hardly characterized by the rapaciousness that makes so many development agencies wary of the private sector.

A second point worth reconsidering is the question of job creation. It was noted that TCC, for reasons of economy and attitude, took a cautious approach to the commonly held view that appropriate and intermediate technology should emphasize job creation. In TCC's view, it should provide employment opportunities which are appropriate to the level of skills, the level of interest, and the level of remunerative expectation of the available labour-force. This is a roundabout way of saying that job creation, at least in the light engineering sector, has been given a low priority by TCC because of prevailing conditions and attitudes in the Ghanaian labour-force.

That said, a few actual numbers can now be examined. On the light engineering side, few of TCC's clients in and around Suame Magazine employ more than a dozen people; most have fewer than half that number. There are about 30 employees at the Suame ITTU. These are not large numbers, given the capital cost of machine tools, but it should be remembered that most of the machine tools will last at least 25 years, which means in the case of the ITTU, 750 person-years of employment, and in the case of Josbarko, with six employees, 150 person-years. Josbarko was established with machine tools and equipment which in 1979 cost 22,500 cedis, or roughly US$8,200, a capital investment (not including land and building which are impossible to estimate) of US$1,363 per work-place, or $54 per person-year of employment. This compares favourably with the 1976 Checchi estimate which indicated an average capital investment of 12,518 cedis (US$10,885) per job created in large-scale industry, 3,304 cedis ($2,638) in shops employing between ten and 30 employees, and 1,100 cedis ($956) in shops with fewer than ten workers.[3]

The longer term employment value from TCC's work with the light engineering sector, however, lies in the products of its clients. For example, four or five broken wheel bolts are enough to cripple a heavy goods vehicle. If Frank Awuah produces 1,000 in a month on his centre lathe, it may represent the continued operation of as many as 200 vehicles. Even allowing 75 per cent room for other work, shut downs and exaggeration, this means that 600 vehicles in a year, critical to the movement of food, crops and other supplies, benefit from Frank Awuah's work in the little shop behind the ITTU. An extrapolation from import data of the 1970s indicates a demand for about a million sets of nuts and bolts a year in Ghana; by 1985, TCC clients were perhaps satisfying 10 per cent of that amount, an important contribution to construction, manufacturing and repair work throughout the country, all of which are significant employers.

In 1984, SIS Engineering produced 202 pieces of machinery, including 30 wood-turning lathes, 60 cassava presses, 15 corn mills and 20 corn/rice hullers. They produced five soap-boiling tanks and five caustic-soda tanks which mean employment for five people each, or the creation of 25 jobs. With a life expectancy of ten years, this means 250 person-years of work. The seven palm-oil presses will occupy three people each for nine months of the year, and over ten years will mean 157 person-years of work. Each of the 12 sawbenches produced in 1984, or the 45 produced in 1983, meant work for two people. While it can be argued that mechanization may have displaced labour, high turnover among hand sawyers is an indication of the unpopularity of this work. But because the sawbenches could use cheap off-cuts from the large sawmills, they increased the supply of cheap raw material, and the number of small sawmills in Anloga actually tripled over a decade.

And for something like fishing boats, the linkages can be traced

112

further. The General Manager of Kofifoh Boatbuilders once said that without the bolts that Joseph Kwaako first found at TCC and then began to produce himself, his boatbuilding would have been seriously curtailed. This would have had its impact not only on jobs for fishermen, but for all those associated with the fishing industry—traders, consumers, animal feed producers, poultry farmers, transporters. Of course, the list of linkages could be drawn out to the point where it is meaningless. However, it is true to say that the indirect job creation effect of TCC's work with the light engineering sector is high, precisely because it *is* a light engineering sector, and because TCC has emphasized production, and more particularly, production of goods which have a high multiplier development effect.

The importation of used machinery from industrialized countries to the Third World is often criticized on practical as well as philosophical grounds. Philosophically, no one wants to be regarded as a dumping ground for second-hand cast-offs. More practically, machinery which may have worked well in one location and under a certain set of circumstances, may behave quite differently when it is shifted; alignments may have changed over the years and other quirks may have developed which are not evident until the new owner takes possession. And a buyer will want to be very sure that value for money is assured; there is no long-term benefit to be gained by paying half price for a machine whose life expectancy is a quarter that of a new one.

The arguments are perhaps not as serious regarding machine tools as they might be with other types of manufacturing equipment. The machine tools that TCC has purchased are basic pieces of equipment, well known throughout the world. As companies in industrialized countries expand and modernize, they tend to move more and more towards semi-automatic or even computer controlled automatic equipment, leaving older, yet serviceable machinery behind. Often, what comes on to the market as used equipment is still relatively new as far as machine tools are concerned. Lathes and milling machines, for example, are built to last for several decades, so even a 20 year old reconditioned machine can have a reasonable life expectancy if properly cared for. The examples in Table 2 from a 1983

113

Table 2

Item	1983 Price (used)	1985 List Price of Similar Machine (new)
7.5″ × 48″ capstan lathe; (1958 model)	£ 550	£ 7,500
Articulated radial arm drill (1960)	850	1,881
Horizontal Milling Machine (1957)	850	12,000
7.5″ × 50″ lathe (1970)	2,350	7,500
Freight and Insurance	1,667	2,500
Total	£6,267	£31,381

(Source: Meggitt Machine Tools & Equipment, Dorset)

order for SIS Engineering gives an idea of the savings that can be achieved.

TCC has learned from experience, however, that care must be taken in ensuring that the supplier is reliable, both in the selection and rehabilitation of machinery, and in the packing and forwarding. A few well-known brand names have been concentrated on, which facilitates maintenance, repairs and the interchangeability of parts, and means that a small stock of tooling and spares, centrally located at TCC, considerably reduces costs and delays.

Foundry work

In 1975, TCC was approached by the Chief of Kurofofurom, a village near Kumasi devoted largely to the production and sale of brass castings. The 'lost wax' method of brass casting is an ancient technique, known in West Africa for hundreds of years. The quality of the work was such that Portuguese slavers centuries ago took people from West Africa to spread the

114

technology in their South American colonies, and the bronzes of ancient Benin and Ife are of such superb classical quality that until recent years, European archaeologists refused to believe that they had not been influenced by ancient Greece and Rome. Such is the international demand for ancient West African bronze castings that in 1985, a single piece from Benin realized £352,000 at a London auction. At Kurofofurom, the work ranged from large decorated urns and traditional Ashanti gold weights, to small figurines and groups of figures representing various scenes and individuals in the village.

The Chief of Kurofofurom was interested in expanding the products that could be made, not least because the market for ornamental objects was fast dwindling, and because he thought there might also be more profitable or useful products that could benefit from the skills available in his village. The idea complemented the light engineering side of TCC's work as well as its interest in rural industries such as beadmaking and weaving, and so various alternatives were examined. One of the shortcomings in the traditional lost wax method is that the wax image of each piece has to be individually made out of beeswax, then encased in a mould of clay and powdered charcoal. As the mould is dried and heated, the wax melts and runs out through a hole in the bottom. Scrap brass encased in another mould is then joined to the first and connected by a small passage. The moulds are heated again and the brass melts, running into the mould that previously held the wax image. When the mould is cooled and opened, a brass image of the original wax figure emerges. The work is time consuming and, as befits an artistic enterprise, there is little uniformity. For potential industrial use, however, these factors were drawbacks, as was the high consumption of charcoal required to heat moulds to the required temperature.

TCC's first consideration was to obtain a product which would maximize income for the villagers, and a number of items were attempted, including door knobs and blanks from which bushings or plumbing fittings could be machined. Tallow added to beeswax improved the quality of castings; plaster of Paris moulds solved the problem of uniformity, and a charcoal-fired kiln was produced at the TCC workshop with

115

bricks made by the Ceramics Section of the UST Department of Industrial Arts. It was hoped that if a cheap, locally made kiln could be produced, higher and better regulated temperatures would be possible, less fuel would be consumed, and it might even be possible to move from the lost wax method to a simple form of sand casting. Progress was exceedingly slow, however. There was, in fact, limited interest in the village in marrying their techniques with modern demands. Scrap brass was becoming more and more scarce, and some of the individuals at the university with relevant experience in casting and ceramics had moved on. Experiments were conducted in aluminium, and a small iron foundry was ordered from Britain, but by 1980 the shortage of diesel fuel to fire the furnace had become a serious impediment to extensive experimentation.

It was not until 1984 that interest in foundry work began to revive. There were several contributing factors. One was the arrival at TCC of Greg Chase, a Peace Corps volunteer with a background in ceramics. Pottery projects were at the basis of his appointment, but he soon took an interest in the Ceramics Section of the Industrial Arts Department, where several kilns

The TCC-designed foundry using palm kernel charcoal, old refractory bricks and a knapsack sprayer engine.

were inoperative for want of refractory bricks. He began to examine possible sources of local clay and kaolin, and soon had enough supplies to attempt some samples with the Department, and to produce a satisfactory refractory cement. At the same time, interest was revived at Suame for a completely different reason. Unlike the situation ten years earlier, there were now a dozen clients operating 60 machine tools in the Magazine, and there were scores of others following the ITTU lead. The demand for scrap steel had risen dramatically, and though the supply seemed enormous, it could not last forever. An alternative was iron. In fact, many items produced by TCC clients used steel because it was available, even though cast iron was more appropriate and was often the material used in the imported models of the machinery being copied. The fact of the matter was that the technology of melting and casting iron was completely unknown. Solomon Adjorlolo's corn grinder was a case in point: several parts on the model he copied were originally cast iron. In an industrialized country, using steel would be unthinkable because of the expense, but in Suame, steel scrap had been plentiful and no one knew how to cast iron.

The tragedy is that iron technology was once commonplace in Ghana, and in fact pre-dated brass casting by more than a thousand years. There are several sites in West Africa where there is evidence of iron extractive industries dating as far back as 500 BC, coinciding almost exactly with the early iron age in Britain. As Basil Davidson put it, the development of the iron age in Africa, 'gave a new mastery over soil and forest . . . and an impulse to conquest and centralized government.' The earliest known sites in Ghana date from the second century AD, and by the 15th century, iron technology had become a folk industry of serious proportions. It was a major factor in agricultural production and population expansion, particularly in the north. Gold technology came later, probably around the 14th century among the Akans, and it was this which drew disproportionate and destructive interest from Europe. Traders from half a dozen European countries flocked to the 'Gold Coast' for the precious metal, and later for ivory and slaves. In return, they brought textiles, firearms, and finished implements

117

made of brass and iron. From the 15th century, under the influence of heavy brass and iron imports, local iron smelting began to die out in the south, although in northern Ghana traditional blacksmiths continued to provide most iron implements and weapons until as late as the 1920s. Instead of producing iron, Ghanaians had become traders in imported finished goods; the only legacy of the country's once flourishing iron age was the availability of scrap brass from imported goods, for recasting in villages like Kurofofurom.

By 1984, scrap steel was no longer plentiful in Suame Magazine, yet scrap iron from more modern binges of importation littered almost every workshop. When roads became impassable in Suame, old engine blocks and crankcases, stripped of everything useful, were thrown into the craters, forming the basis of some of the main roads. It was not exactly gold, but the iron was only waiting for the technology to arrive. It had actually arrived several years earlier at the ITTU in the form of the small iron foundry that had been ordered from Britain. It used diesel fuel, however, and even a copy would consume large amounts of imported materials, so work began on a viable local alternative. A model was tested with brass, using an old oil drum and discarded refractory bricks from the Obuasi gold mine, and a few large castings were produced. Gradually, an approach evolved. A larger steel drum was produced in the workshop. Old refractory bricks were used, along with Greg Chase's first batch of refractory cement. Palm-kernel charcoal, a traditional high-grade charcoal well known to Ghanaian blacksmiths, was used as the fuel. And for bellows, a small petrol-driven blower was fabricated out of a knapsack sprayer engine, of the sort commonly used to spray insecticide on cocoa trees. And in May 1985, a 20 kg charge of scrap iron was melted and poured, to the amazement of 50 Suame fitters who watched the process with interest and enthusiasm.

Small iron foundries are common throughout Asia, but in West Africa's informal sector, the technology is completely unknown, so it was something of a breakthrough. For although one or two large iron foundries had been encouraged by government, a technique that was within reach of the

TCC in the headlines: Daily Graphic, May 6, 1985.

119

informal industrial sector was important, both to an effective industrial revolution, and to a country which could make much more effective use of recycled scrap. The media recognized the significance of what had been achieved. Ghana's largest newspaper, the *Graphic*, gave the story a front page headline: 'ITTU Engineers Achieve Another Feat.' The report said that the event had 'opened the way to the recycling of the thousands of tons of scrap iron scattered all over the Suame Magazine and various parts of the country and this could save the economy millions of dollars over the next few years.'[4] Not to be outdone, the *Ghanaian Times* headline the same day was 'Palm Kernel Powers Steel Furnace'. Although the reporter had confused steel with iron, an editorial on page 2 was far from confused: 'Engineers of the Suame ITTU . . . represent classic examples of what a determined people can do for themselves . . . what we find commendable is that the engineers did not see the manufacture of the furnaces alone as the end of their job, but researched into the use of palm kernel as an alternative source of energy . . . the beautiful advantage is that it is going to be easy to transfer the technology to every nook and corner of the country.'[5]

It was flattering praise, but if the development of a simple technology was the same as transferring it to every nook and corner of the country, a hundred TCC ideas that had died on the vine would today be flourishing industries. It is more likely that the development of the furnace will take time; additives will be required before a suitable recycled iron is found for some products. Workshops that know steel will have to learn the new technology; SIS Engineering will have to see and feel the advantage in redesigning its product, in retraining workers, in obtaining new tooling and developing new customers. Despite the obvious value of what had occurred, a demand would have to be created, and the right price would have to be found, not only for the end user, but for the producer. It would have to be more than 'affordable' and more than 'economically viable'; it would have to be profitable. And the industrial revolution in Suame will, in a sense, have to move back a stage, from steel to iron, to *production* from iron, rather than fabrication from bending and machining and welding steel. But in a sense, the *Times* was right: TCC did represent, through its successful clients and their products—the wheel bolts, the piston rings, the corn mills, a hundred resuscitated Volkswagens —classic examples of what a determined people can do for themselves. Those who say there is no development in Africa would change their minds after a day in Suame Magazine.

CHAPTER 8
Scrap into Ploughshares

Like most who make the 30 kilometre journey south of Kumasi to Lake Bosomtwe, Francis Oduro-Boateng, an impressionable young high-school student, was unprepared for what he saw when he neared the edge of the crater at Abonu in the summer of 1967. Spread out in the mist below him was one of the most magnificent sights in Ghana: nestled in a huge crater 8 kilometres across, lay a hidden lake, almost perfectly round. The lake, well known in Ashanti legend, was said to have moved itself from a location 160 kilometres to the north after a dispute with certain river gods. The Golden Stool, symbol of Ashanti culture and power, was said to have descended to earth at Lake Bosomtwe. An ancient taboo against metal prevented the use of aluminium boats, motors, and even fish hooks in the lake, and it was said that Bosomtwe was virtually bottomless; one American surveyor had reportedly tested it to a depth of 230 metres and still not found bottom. No one seemed to know whether the lake, unique in West Africa, was of meteoric, volcanic or spiritual origin. The water was brackish, and every year or so, a strange thing happened: fish in their thousands would die in a single night and float to the surface. The local people said they were a gift from the lake god, and great efforts were made to ensure his happiness. As Francis Oduro-Boateng made his way down the overgrown path that led to the shore of the lake, he had some of these tales in mind, and although he did not know it at the time, he and the lake were in the process of forming a lasting attachment.

Years later, Oduro-Boateng majored in freshwater biology at the University of Science and Technology, and then, because of his interest in the lake, he went on to study limnology and aquaculture at the Italian Institute of Hydro Biology. In 1980, he was back at Bosomtwe, looking into the possibility of commercial fishing on the lake. At that time, there were probably about 18,000 people living in two dozen villages inside the rim of the crater, and fishing provided at least half of them with both food and a livelihood. By then, a number of things had changed at Bosomtwe. For one thing, there was a paved road where Oduro-Boateng had first been forced to walk. For another, the ancient taboo against metal on the lake had been lifted by the Asantehene six years earlier. And although the body of research that existed on Bosomtwe was not large, a number of facts had been established. The lake, formed by meteoric impact a million and a half years ago, was not bottomless; at the centre it was 78 metres in depth. Although the water contained an appreciable amount of sulphate and chloride which made it undrinkable, the lake supported 11 varieties of fish, the most important of which was the *tilapia discolor*.

Because of the importance of fishing to the villagers and the declining catch, Oduro-Boateng decided on a plan. He went to TCC in Kumasi and asked for assistance in approaching the International Federation for Science in Stockholm; in 1982, they agreed to finance his project if TCC would administer it. His ultimate objective was the introduction of cage culture for the *T-discolor*, which would involve the development of suitable breeding techniques, construction of durable floating cages and the production of an inexpensive, locally produced fish feed. The overriding objective was that all the work had to be done using technologies that were within the technical and economic means of the Bosomtwe villages.

TCC provided him with administrative assistance and a Land Rover for the daily journey to Bosomtwe and back, and gradually the project took shape. Because the lake is sustained by rain and by spring-fed streams that run only inwards, the level of the lake has been rising by about 30 cm a year, which meant that hand-dug breeding ponds near the shore could be filled by seepage rather than pumps. Five brood fish were put into each of six ponds, and within six months, 1,600 fingerlings averaging 4 cm in length were produced, yielding a considerable profit over the cost of digging and maintaining the ponds.

A series of floating fish cages were constructed using wood

123

for the frame, and raffia, waterproofed with tar, for the bars, bound together with copper wire and attached to a raft of wood and bamboo. The whole structure was anchored in place, appropriately enough, with an old engine block from Suame Magazine. Oduro-Boateng found that a cage could hold over 250 fish during the rearing season, and at 10 cedis for a single fish of 20 cm, the economic indicators of the project showed great potential. He also discovered that using cow pea and groundnut cake as a substitute for the fishmeal component of a standard feed, that growth rates of the fish were similar, yet feed costs were reduced by 35 per cent. Because the economics of cage culture depend largely on the cost of supplemental feed, this was an important discovery.

The actual transfer of what Francis Oduro-Boateng learns lies in the future, as does a solution to the sudden-death syndrome that strikes the lake every year or so. Oduro-Boateng saw it happen in 1983, and fortunately had enough laboratory equipment and chemicals with him the day it occurred to offer a scientific explanation. It was an abrupt and alarming drop in the oxygen level of the lake that caused the fish to die, a condition that lingered for three days, along with an increase in hydrogen sulphide. Because the lake has no outlet, the level of algae is always very high, and at night, when plant absorption of oxygen is at its greatest, the oxygen level in the lake drops. If it falls below a certain point, it not only begins to kill the fish, the dead algae produce hydrogen sulphide, adding to the problem. In other countries where fish farming is common, this problem can be solved with pumps aerating the water around the cages, but on Bosomtwe, if locally available resources are to be used, this is an unlikely answer to a problem that the local people see as a gift from the gods.

A gift from the government, or lack thereof, was what stymied another fishing project with which TCC was involved in Kumasi itself. In 1982, the government introduced a drive to establish fish farming throughout the country, and said that institutions such as UST should lead the way. With the assistance of Francis Oduro-Boateng, TCC built a half-acre pond on a farm near the campus and introduced five species of tilapia, three of them from Bosomtwe. During the terrible drought of 1983 when new fish ponds across Ghana were drying up, TCC's flourished, and samples showed that the fish were breeding and healthy. The problem, however, was the almost complete absence in Ghana of nets for harvesting the ponds. TCC managed on occasion to hire one, but the problems experienced by a large well-known institution in this regard would be nothing compared to the agony that a farmer would experience. It was a case not unlike some from the early years at TCC when a simple technology showed tremendous potential and had seemed undeniably appropriate, yet failed because of a single missing ingredient.

Although TCC's primary emphasis was always on the light engineering sector, agriculture was never far from its thinking, both indirectly, in the products produced by Suame clients, and more directly in its contact with farmers and with organizations working in agricultural production. Agriculture accounts for more than half of Ghana's gross domestic product. Staples include maize, rice, millet, yams, cassava and plantain. Some of the indigenous crops, such as millet, West African rice and guinea corn, were taken to the New World by the Portuguese, while pineapple, groundnuts and cassava were brought back. The oil palm was an essential part of both subsistence and export economies, but nothing matched cocoa, either in its importance or in its meteoric rise. In 1879, Tetteh Quarshie, a native of Mampong in the Akwapim Hills, brought some cocoa seeds back from a trip to the Portuguese colony of Fernando Po. Although they grew well, and the government encouraged nurseries and plantations, it would have been hard to predict in 1891, when the first tentative exports left the country, that Ghana would one day become the world's largest producer of cocoa.

In Ghana today, almost three-quarters of the population is directly involved in agriculture or related activities, mostly on small farms of less than three acres, usually composed of several non-contiguous fields. Traditionally, there may once have been an equal division of labour between men and women, but with the introduction of cash crops such as cocoa, women—especially in the south of Ghana—have taken the larger share of the burden in producing food crops. Generally, men clear the land and fell trees, while planting, weeding, harvesting, and carrying the crops home is done largely by the women, who are also responsible for almost all of the subsequent food processing, marketing and storage. In northern Ghana the pattern differs; there women concentrate largely on planting and processing. But in the south, among the matrilineal Akans, which include Ashantis, Akims, Akwapims, Brong Ahafos and Fantis, when a man dies, it is his family on his mother's side—his nephews and nieces—who inherit what he owned. It is therefore the wife's enterprise, work and savings that will generally provide her and her children with whatever future security they are to have.

Food production in Ghana stagnated or declined throughout the 1970s; production in 1980 was 75 per cent of what it had been five years earlier, and about 10 to 15 per cent of the annual cereal consumption, mostly maize and rice, was being imported. As with almost every other sector of the economy, the blame could be attributed to a number of factors: droughts in 1975–7 and again in 1982–3, poor transportation facilities, inadequate support services, lack of foreign exchange for the purchase of fertilizer and other inputs, and policies which favoured large farmers and ignored the small. In Nkrumah's time, industrialization was intended to fuel the supply of equipment to and demand from the agricultural sector, which in itself underwent heavy investment in mechanization. This was not unusual, for in the 1950s and 1960s, agricultural mechanization was a generally accepted route to increased food production, although in Ghana it was learned the hard way that neither mechanization nor the creation of State Farms were sufficient in themselves to improve production.

If anything, the State Farms absorbed most of the government's competent agriculturalists, thus heightening the contrast between the modern and traditional sectors, a contrast that had been the butt of one of Nkrumah's main criticisms of the colonial regime. Hampered by lack of support systems, as well as forward and backwards linkages, by damaged soil, lack of foreign exchange for fuel, parts and chemicals, and by political interference, the State Farms were a disaster as far as food crops were concerned.

126

Table 3: Yields[1]

	Peasants	State Farms
Maize	0.49	0.26
Rice	0.49	0.13
Yams	2.63	1.68
Groundnuts	0.40	0.18

(1964–70; Tons per Acre)

The Acheampong government of the 1970s will be remembered in Ghana for its 'Operation Feed Yourself', which developed a measure of enthusiasm for food farming and managed to get some credit and equipment to small farmers. But the bulk of the resources were still skewed towards large-scale mechanical rice farming in the north. In the four years between 1970 and 1975, for example, more than 140 combine harvesters and over 2,000 tractors were imported into Ghana. The Third Republic's 'New Deal' in agriculture operated with the same stacked deck as the old, once again ignoring the small farmer. Travelling through the countryside, hundreds of tractors and combines, each one an expensive investment in Ghana's future, can be seen half cannibalized, parked where they finally came to rest years before. And yet one of the rarest sights is an abandoned bicycle or bullock plough. In this, there is an obvious lesson which is not a thousand miles removed from the central theme of this book, and it has to do with choices of technology.

Band saws into cutlasses

Basically, there are three types of agricultural mechanization in Ghana: the farmer with a hoe and cutlass practising slash-and-burn, shifting cultivation, usually on about 2.5 acres of land; the farmer with bullock-drawn equipment who can usually manage about 10 acres; and those with four-wheeled equipment such as tractors and combine harvesters. It is estimated that despite all the investment in mechanization, 90 per cent of Ghana's food production still comes from the small-scale

127

farmer. Of these, there are probably about a million in Ghana (Buchele & Campbell estimated 900,000 in 1975),[2] and though many may eventually graduate to higher forms of technology and agricultural practices, soil conditions in Ghana are such that the hoe and cutlass will probably remain the basic technology for about half the arable land.

This does not mean, however, that there is no room for modernization; far from it. Ghana's rapidly growing population, estimated at 12 million in 1982 and expected to reach 24 million by the year 2000, demands it. Since the bulk of Ghana's food production is still derived from the small farmer, the obvious place for TCC attention was in this area, with a view to increasing output and improving the productivity of labour. There were various ways the subject could have been approached, although any creative design work had to take into consideration the people it would affect, soil conditions, local infrastructure, farm size and topography, and would require the same consideration of design and material that would be offered in the light engineering sector. As Schumacher once pointed out, using low carbon steel for a plough when the technology of high carbon steel is available only penalizes the farmer and shows a disregard for existing knowledge.

In Ghana, however, much work had already been done on innovative design at various research institutions and universities, with no appreciable effect. Part of the problem was a concentration on the design of mechanical devices with little consideration of prevailing conditions in rural areas. The system into which a device was supposed to fit was often ignored, and back up support systems—marketing, service, extension, credit facilities—often created serious bottlenecks. An example of the problem was a grain storage silo developed by one of the faculties at UST. It was made entirely of easily available material—plywood, wire, a few nails and some paint—and was intended to reduce the spoilage of maize considerably. Under ideal conditions, it worked well, but one of these conditions was the occasional attachment at its base of a motorized blower to ensure a constant, low moisture content. This was, needless to say, a rare item away from the campus. A second problem was the plywood, which did not

128

stand up well to the rainy season. Field tests revealed high levels of spoilage. The answer was somewhat impractical: the silo, over ten feet high, should be kept indoors.

A more realistic approach was taken by TCC to a request for hoes, one of the Centre's first forays into farming. Several Catholic and Protestant mission stations in the north of Ghana were actively involved in agriculture and they approached TCC when a shortage of imported hoes and cutlasses began to affect their work. Some 200 cutlasses and 1,000 hoes were produced by TCC from used sawmill blades and truck leaf-springs, but in the case of the latter, they were sent to the north without handles and untempered; local blacksmiths and carpenters could add the handles and shape the implements to suit local tastes and conditions, a fundamental prerequisite to acceptance.

In a classic example of appropriate technology, many of the mission stations across Ghana's Northern and Upper Regions became heavily involved in the introduction of bullock traction as an intermediary between traditional slash and burn farming, and the highly mechanized modern plant being encouraged by government policies. They found that the acceptance level among farmers was high, but as foreign exchange dwindled, it became as difficult to get an imported bullock plough as a tractor. They had relied heavily on a British designed plough imported from Nigeria, and when these started to break down, the missions asked TCC for assistance. Insufficient quantities of hard steel prevented the complete manufacture of a plough at TCC workshops, but it was discovered that old ploughs could be refurbished and repaired, often with improvements. The cast iron wheel, for example, was one of the first things to break, and proved to be an example of how Ghana's lack of iron technology actually worked in the farmers' favour. Replacement wheels, of which hundreds were made, had to be fabricated from more durable scrap steel which, unlike the brittle iron, rebounded unscathed from rocks and other obstacles. A replaceable bushing was also developed which prolonged the life of the wheel and made local repairs possible.

Growth in the use of bullock traction soon created a demand

129

for other equipment that could be moved by animal traction; one of the mission stations, for example, asked TCC for assistance in the development of a bullock cart. Undoubtedly there is much duplication of effort among AT institutions, and perhaps a case can be made for the need in each country to re-invent the wheel before it will be accepted. But happily in the case of the bullock cart, it was known that the Tanzanian Agricultural Machinery Testing Unit (TAMTU) had already developed successful bullock and donkey carts. Designs eventually arrived and in 1976, TCC-produced models were sent north for testing. The results were positive, and a formula was established where TCC fabricated the metal parts in Kumasi and then sent them north where they could be assembled together with locally produced wooden components.

Another early agricultural venture resulted from a lengthy survey of the north by TCC's Deputy Director, Ben Ntim. One of the biggest problems in introducing new crops, such as rice in the north, or a new technology such as animal traction, is sorting out the inevitable bottlenecks that can result. Can a farmer plant an area big enough and quickly enough to make bullock traction worthwhile? Can farmers plant more than they can harvest? Can they harvest more than they can weed or transport, or process or store? Rice production had grown so rapidly in northern Ghana, for example, that a bottleneck was occurring at the threshing stage. About 60 per cent of all rice was being produced by small farmers, who threshed it by beating the rice on the ground with sticks. Because of the time it took, the rice was often dry and brittle, the resulting product usually contained sand, and was often so badly broken that it was fit for little more than poultry feed. An obvious mechanical solution was the importation of even more tractors and combine harvesters, but by now, the foreign exchange problem had removed the bloom from that rose. Ntim had another idea.

With assistance from the International Rice Research Institute in the Philippines and lessons learned from a Chinese pedal thresher that TCC had been asked to repair, a model was designed to meet local conditions. Like the Chinese model, it was pedal driven and used simple bicycle technology—pedals,

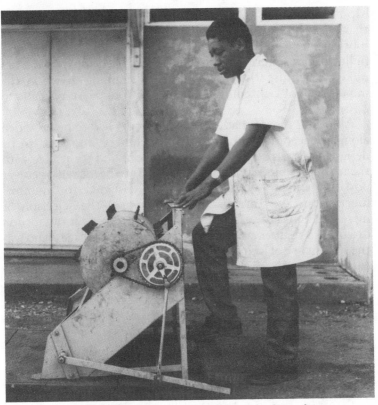

A prototype rice thresher using a bicycle chain drive.

sprockets and two chain drives—that would be well known and easily repaired even in remote northern villages. Initial support for the project was provided by USAID, and subsequently by the International Development Research Centre in Ottawa. Through the production and testing of several prototypes and dozens of field models, a number of defects were gradually eliminated, although one fundamental lesson was learned. Despite widespread use of the bicycle, repairs, especially in the north, were not easy to obtain. Shops advertising repair facilities could often do little more than patch a tyre, and under farm conditions the situation was even more troublesome.

Most farmers were not familiar with anything more complicated than the hoe and cutlass, and simple concepts such as lubrication of moving parts, whether on a rice thresher or a bullock cart, were unknown. Bolts often dropped from ploughs because there had been no training given in the importance of tightening them, and no tools were available to do so.

All of this meant that improved training had to be provided along with equipment, but that machinery, too, had to be designed to withstand rugged conditions and to survive with the least possible maintenance; nuts had to be locked wherever possible, moving parts had to be designed for minimal lubrication, and care had to be taken in the selection of materials. In the case of the rice thresher, it was soon discovered that it was the blacksmith in most villages who was the repository of knowledge about machinery, and he had little experience with bearings and chains. When one of the two chains on the thresher broke or slipped off, resynchronizing it with the other proved difficult, and the results were misaligned axles, seized bearings and broken machines. Redesigning the machine for a single-chain drive was not a significant improvement, and TCC began to discover just how complicated bicycle technology actually was, despite its widespread use. Recent models of the thresher have switched to a more sturdy gear drive.

Apart from the technical difficulties, TCC also ran into other delays. The rice thresher was intended for use in the north, and it was assumed that the Tamale ITTU was the logical centre for production and field testing. With the start of USAID assistance in 1979, the Tamale ITTU seemed only a matter of months from opening, but as the months dragged into years, prospects for early volume production of the rice thresher receded. The Tamale ITTU building and equipment were finally erected and installed in 1985, and so a decade after the first prototype of the rice thresher was developed, volume production was perhaps in sight.

Pipes into presses

In 1976, TCC turned its attention to palm oil. Palm oil was the main ingredient in the TCC soapmaking process (described in Chapter 9, and inflation was adding significantly to its cost. A large part of the cost of palm oil could be found in slow and inefficient traditional techniques of extraction. Traditionally, women boil the palm fruit, cool it overnight and then pound it the following day in a vat to which water has been added. The resulting liquid is again boiled and the water siphoned off. There are several problems with the technique, however, not least of which is the tremendous demand the work places on women's time and energy, not only for gathering, cooking, pounding and boiling the oil, but in obtaining fuel for what is essentially an energy-intensive process. In addition, yields are much lower than they might be, as the pounding is a much less efficient extraction technique than compression.

The first step in developing a new process was an oil press which could reduce the amount of time involved, and increase the yield of oil. The design was an adaptation of one used in Sierra Leone, made from a section of used steel pipe, 32.5 cm in diameter, with a piston moving on a screw in the centre of the cylinder and fixed to a bottom plate. The boiled fruit was placed in the press and two workers on either end of a long handle screwed the piston downward, expelling the oil from holes in the sides of the cylinder. The first model was improved by producing the cylinder in two parts, held together by a simple locking pin and hinge, but easily opened for access to the crushed fruit and for cleaning. In the late 1970s, dozens of oil presses were manufactured, and a case study of a small plantation carried out in 1978,[3] showed that the cost of palm oil production using the TCC press was roughly half the market price of oil, providing a significant margin over the cost of traditional techniques.

A common failing of AT institutions is their concentration on research and development, often re-inventing at great cost machinery and techniques that are already well known. Although TCC has perhaps re-invented a few wheels in its time, it tries not to, and views its purpose not so much in the

133

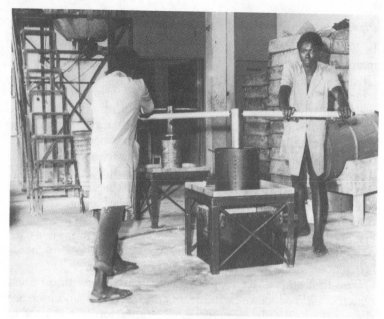

A TCC palm oil press in use.

development of new technologies, as in the identification of known solutions to existing problems, and their application. When Frank Robertson first went to Tamale, he was particularly galled to see women lugging water all day from wells in the city. He was upset because knowledge of water pressure and the technology of piped delivery systems have been known for two thousand years. He knew, however, that there was more to the transfer of technology than simply having 'access' to it. Even in the case of simple water technologies, money, influence, knowledge and skills all play a part. Adaptation of known technologies to local materials, labour and social conditions, and to available machinery and equipment are required before a new idea can be successfully introduced.

What this meant for TCC was not so much product research and development—invention—as product adaptation to suit local conditions and attitudes. The Tanzanian bullock cart,

134

the Kenya top-bar beehive, minimum tillage agriculture from Nigeria and the Sierra Leone oil press were all examples of this. A 'new' oil press 'invented' in the Cameroon in 1985, and expected to have a major impact there on costs of production, labour, and so on, illustrates the point. The press was smaller than the one TCC had developed, and relied on a car jack rather than a screw for its pressure. The Cameroon model, still in the prototype stage, was estimated to cost US$254 and in a six-hour day could produce 240 kg of palm oil.[4] The TCC press was being produced at SIS Engineering at that time for the equivalent of US$490, but could produce 600 kg in a six-hour day, giving it a 29 per cent cost/production advantage over the Cameroon model. Of course, the Cameroon model may have suited local conditions well, especially in the absence of a machine shop like SIS Engineering, and in a country where used car jacks are available for about US$25. In Ghana, however, a similar jack would have cost over US$90, and would have made the Cameroon model even less attractive. The real point of comparison, however, was that in Ghana, SIS Engineering did exist, thanks to TCC, and as a result, a more cost effective production-line oil press, locally made and independent of the imported car jack, was being produced.

A press was only part of the solution to reducing the cost of oil production, however, for the largest costs were still associated with the excessive use of fuel for boiling, and with the high amounts of human energy and time required for pounding the boiled fruit. Gradually, one idea followed another. More energy-efficient boiling tanks were a short step from tanks TCC was already manufacturing for soap production; a pounding machine was developed by SIS Engineering, and a palm-kernel cracking machine was also produced. One of the largest customers for the equipment was the National Council on Women and Development which purchased items or complete sets of equipment for the establishment of rural co-operatives and for service centres where women could bring their fruit and take advantage of the new technology at a reasonable price.

The NCWD, along with other development agencies and mission stations in the north, were important to the creation of a demand for other food processing equipment, but more so for getting it into the hands of women. All too often, new technologies are programmed through men's co-operatives or through male entrepreneurs. However, in Ghana, since food processing and marketing is traditionally within the purview of women, strong efforts have been made to ensure that new technologies stay with women. Gari, for example, once the staple food of the Volta Region, is now widespread in popularity, but consumes vast amounts of female labour in its preparation. Cassava is peeled and grated by hand, a time-consuming process which is hard on the hands. The mash is then put into sacks and weighed down with stones to expel water and excess starch, and after two or three days is roasted and prepared for consumption or sale. With TCC assistance, SIS Engineering produced a cassava grater, a simple and inexpensive press—of which they sold 60 in 1984 alone—and an energy efficient roaster. Many of these machines have been programmed through the NCWD and other development organizations. On occasion, men have become involved, setting up small commercial gari processing or corn milling centres. Since women control both the supply of the raw material and the marketing of it, however, these middlemen have in most cases acted to their advantage. Many women who have neither their own machines nor access to a co-operative, take cassava to such centres, wait while it is processed, and then take it to market where their net income still reflects a more cost-effective use of their time and energy than reliance on traditional methods.

Down on the farm

Most of TCC's work in agriculture and food processing would never have been possible without the light engineering capability developed first on the UST campus and later at Suame Magazine. The demand for agricultural equipment was, in some cases, well established, and had previously been satisfied through imports or *kalebule*. In other cases it was latent, as in the case of palm-oil equipment, the impetus for which came not from women who specialized in processing oil, but from other women using the TCC soap production

136

method and feeling the downward pressure of market forces on their product. As will be seen in Chapter 10, the development of beekeeping at TCC was spurred not so much by the potential market for honey, which later dominated the project, but by an early interest in more and better quality beeswax for the brass-casters of Kurofofurom. For the purposes of this narrative, some of the products and techniques developed at TCC have been isolated, but in actual fact few, if any, of the Centre's endeavours over the years have been developed in complete isolation from other projects. More than anything else, it is probably this highly integrated nature of TCC's work, along with the continuity and the memory provided by senior staff, which has made the Centre unique.

Agriculture, representing over 50 per cent of the gross domestic product and involving three-quarters of the population of Ghana, was obviously an important area for TCC involvement. However, through the 1970s, most efforts sprang from the light engineering side of the work, usually in response to random requests rather than a planned strategy. This began to change in September 1978, when Kwesi Opoku-Debrah, former National Serviceman and afterwards a TCC Research Fellow, visited the International Institute for Tropical Agriculture in Nigeria. The IITA had for several years been carrying out experiments in what it called 'zero tillage'—an effort to increase food production without damaging the ecology and without putting more strain on the farm family. It had long been known that mechanized ploughing in West Africa had serious deleterious effects on the soil. Erosion, hardening of the lateritic soils, leaching and oxidation reduced yields dramatically within two or three years, requiring heavy inputs of fertilizer if the land was to be kept in production. This in turn led to further problems, not least of which was pollution of hitherto potable water supplies. In Ghana, it was estimated that only 20 per cent of the arable land was suitable for mechanized farming and that as much as 47 per cent was unsuitable for anything more than variations on traditional hoe and cutlass farming. Ironically, the land which had supported magnificent forests for thousands of years was weak, and without a great deal of care, could not long sustain even a field of maize once it had felt the bite of modern technology.

IITA had returned to basics and decided that a first premise involved as little disturbance of the soil as possible, from clearing and planting through weeding, to harvest. The basic approach that eventually emerged was simple: weed and crop residue would be left on the surface, and new crops would be planted through it. The cycle began by spraying with a herbicide to clear the land, planting straight through the resulting mulch; spraying again for weeds and pests, and possibly doing a small amount of hand weeding; fertilizing and finally, harvesting. Despite the need for sprays and fertilizers, there were two things which encouraged IITA to develop the zero tillage approach: the first was labour. Traditional farming in West Africa is back-breaking work, and if increased food production was to be achieved without the human dislocations, the ecological ravages and the insupportable costs associated with mechanized farming, a new approach which met both the moral and the material aspirations of small farmers had to be found. The second was erosion. Regardless of the short-term economics of mechanized farming, the long-term toll on most land was incalculable. Zero tillage addressed both problems. IITA found that it reduced labour requirements by an incredible factor of more than 150, and produced results that were almost as startling on erosion. Planting maize on a 10 per cent slope, for example, IITA scientists discovered that erosion under zero tillage was one-fortieth of that using conventional tillage.[5] Even on a 15 per cent slope, there was virtually no erosion.

Kwesi Opoku-Debrah returned to Kumasi full of enthusiasm for what he had learned and seen at IITA. Coincidentally, Frank Lukey, long-time friend and associate of TCC, had been working on a PhD thesis which postulated that population pressure in the Ashanti Region would absorb all arable land by the year 2000, but that increasing urban drift would lead to agricultural labour problems and inadequate food production unless higher yields and greater productivity were achieved. Working on the premise that foreign exchange would be insufficient even to partially mechanize the agriculture sector

138

Table 4: Comparative Labour Requirements for Field Preparation Conventional vs. Zero Tillage[6]

| Labour Requirements | PERSON HOURS PER HECTARE | |
	Zero Tillage	Conventional
Slash and burn; then till manually	–	180
Spraying with systemic herbicide	5	–
Seeding; manual vs. injection planter	15	20
Manual weed control (twice) vs. spraying	5	280
Hand fertilizing vs. hand-propelled band application	6	25
Insecticide vs. knapsack spraying	2	10
Total number of hours for field preparation:	33	515

as an alternative, and curious about the zero tillage idea brought back from Nigeria by Kwesi Opoku-Debrah, he decided to make the pilgrimage to IITA himself. He returned to Ghana, like Saul on the road to Damascus, convinced that an answer to the country's food problem, and more particularly the labour problem, had been found.

At TCC they called it minimum tillage or 'minimum till' farming, and a pilot project was initiated in 1981. A pig farmer agreed to loan ten acres of his land to TCC for maize production, on the condition that he could purchase as much maize as he wanted at harvest time, at the prevailing farm-gate price. Kwesi Opoku-Debrah ran the project much as he had seen it done at IITA. First he sprayed with Gramoxone, a well known herbicide that had been available in Ghana for years;

this contained the active chemical, Paraquat, the safety of which was considered in a 1981 study, commissioned by TCC.[7] Unlike the IITA reports, Opoku-Debrah found that some hoeing and weeding was necessary, but the net requirement was infinitely less laborious than doing all the work by hand.

The maize was planted using a rotary planter adapted by TCC—from an IITA design—essential both for the straight line it produced and for the appropriate spacing of seeds. Fertilizing was done at the same time, either using the planter beside the seed rows or by hand. The maize required some thinning, and then, about three weeks after planting, a

Minimum tillage farming: the rotary punch planter injects seeds through the mulch.

pesticide was used to prevent stem-borer infestation. Five weeks after planting, when the maize was about half a metre in height, the field was weeded using a combination of dilute Gramoxone on heavy problem areas, and a hoe for the rest. Although it had taken more work than IITA's theoretical studies had indicated, the results were excellent. A yield of five bags of maize per acre is regarded as reasonable in the Kumasi area, but Kwesi Opoku-Debrah took 122 bags off his ten acres, a yield of more than 12 bags per acre. The result was so good that Opoku-Debrah decided to become a farmer himself, a sure sign that the teacher not only understood his subject, but believed in it. Like other TCC staff before him, Opoku-Debrah was, overnight, transformed from staff member to client. He and four partners established a small farm called 'Approtech', not far from the UST campus, and since 1982, various crops and experiments have been attempted, often with TCC assistance.

All the discussion of herbicides and pesticides at Approtech farm would probably be enough to completely desiccate the average organic farmer, for indeed, minimum till farming is far from an organic approach. The use of chemicals is seen as a means to an end, however, and if a successful mulching regime can be established, the need for herbicides and fertilizer should decline in the second or third year of planting. The bottom line, however, in a hostile climate where farmers—half of them women—fight the most destructive insects, weeds and diseases known, is increased production and reduced labour requirements, using known inputs and minimal foreign exchange requirements. No one who has cleared land and invested savings in seed, only to see the whole thing disappear in an infestation of stem-borers, will be very interested in theories about organic methods of controlling insects unless proof positive is available at first hand.

That said, however, attempts are being made to reduce dependence on chemicals. In 1985, an experiment in 'alley cropping' began, using both *Gliricidia*, a local leguminous tree, and imported *Leucaena*, well known throughout Asia as 'ipil-ipil'. Both trees grow very quickly, and planted between the rows of maize, their leaves form an excellent mulch if the

141

saplings are cropped just before the rains. They kill weeds by blocking out sunlight, they recycle nitrogen and maintain moisture in the soil, thus reducing the need for fertilizer and herbicide. In addition to these experiments, chaya, a Central American shrub which produces a high protein, spinach-like leaf—year round—was introduced. And experiments using leaves from the neem tree as an insect repelling mulch for maize began.

It would have been unnatural, and unlike any other TCC endeavour, had there been no problems. Chaya was difficult to handle and caused skin irritation; besides, cocoa yam leaves were similar, well known and freely available. It did not matter that chaya had almost three times the protein. Then, in 1984, Kwesi Opoku-Debrah was offered an overseas scholarship, and the harvest that year was unmemorable as a result of his departure. One weed was resistant to general Gramoxone spraying, and hoeing only seemed to encourage it further, requiring special, more intensive applications of the herbicide. The *Leucaena* proved superior to the local *Gliricidia* as a mulch, but only 20 per cent of the *Leucaena* seeds, which had a 98 per cent germination rate under nursery conditions, sprouted in the field. And there were problems in the handling of both herbicides and pesticides. This had little to do with TCC, for the sprays had been known and used in Ghana for years, but it was disturbing to find that they were often transported in recycled drinks bottles, while their original containers were in demand as water carriers and for storage of palm oil.

By 1985, over 100 hectares of farm-land in the Kumasi area was using minimum till techniques, thanks to the TCC effort. Training and publicity will play an important part in widening the acceptance of the technology, and to this end the Approtech farm was used to train upwards of 100 farmers in its first two years of operation. In addition, one of the Approtech farmworkers purchased a rotary planter for himself in 1985 and began to undertake contract spraying and planting for farmers who were either uncertain of the technology, or could not afford to purchase a planter themselves. And training was also being given on the care and handling of herbicides and pesticides. Long-term success in minimum till farming and alley cropping in Ghana, however, will depend largely on economics. There is little hard data on the Ghanaian experience to date, but there is no doubt at TCC that it is significantly cheaper, both for the farmer and—in terms of foreign exchange and long-term benefits in increased food production and reduced erosion—for the nation.

CHAPTER 9

No Accounting for Taste

This chapter and the one following—A Taste of Honey—deal in some depth with two specific projects. Chapter 10 considers a relatively new TCC enterprise, beekeeping, while this chapter concerns one of the Centre's longest-running projects, soapmaking. The story of TCC's involvement in soapmaking is, in essence, the story of appropriate technology in Ghana, for the ups and downs of the project run the gamut of TCC's experience of light industry, rural co-operatives, clients, government, the university, and all of the brickbats that could be thrown at it by an unpredictable economy, by the intervention of a transnational corporation, by corruption and an interplay of societal values that would confound an army of marketing experts. It is also a vivid demonstration of the way in which one TCC project impinged on many others, and how everything in creation tended to impinge on the enterprise at hand. 'Soap and education are not as sudden as a massacre,' wrote Mark Twain, 'but they are more deadly in the long run.' In the case of TCC, soap and education were, over the years, to become almost synonymous.

Soapmaking is one of the oldest industries in the world. In pre-Roman Europe, people mixed animal fat with ashes containing potash in order to produce a crude cleansing material. The Romans probably learned the art from the Phoenicians or the Gauls, or from the Celts who called it 'saipo', and by the Middle Ages, vegetable oils were being used in place of tallow. The mediaeval Italian town of Savona, an early commercial soap production centre, gave soap its Romance name—'savon', 'sabon', 'jabon', but it was not until the discovery of a chemical process for the manufacture of caustic soda in the 18th century that soapmaking was placed on a scientific footing. When W.H. Lever introduced Sunlight

Soap to Britain in 1884, he was well on the way to dominating a soap industry that would soon create an immense demand for tropical vegetable oils from West Africa. Ironically, in West Africa, the development of soapmaking was not dissimilar to the European pattern, although several of the intermediate stages were omitted. When the Portuguese first arrived on the coast of Ghana at the end of the 15th century, they found a soap made from palm oil blended with a potash derived from wood ashes. In 1963, the same basic methodology could be found in most Ghanaian villages, but it was in that year that the successor to W.H. Lever, now a giant transnational manufacturing concern, opened the doors of its soap manufacturing plant in the port city of Tema.

Operating in Ghana would be less than ideal for Lever Brothers, although as part of a complex of manufacturing concerns, the soap factory could presumably operate at an occasional loss without affecting the overall profitability of the company. Working to full capacity, with three shifts and 750 employees, the Tema factory was capable of producing 30,000 tons of soap annually, which would account for about half of the country's annual demand. In the 1970s, however, the soap plant frequently found itself starved of raw materials, and production fluctuated according to the availability of import licences and foreign exchange. Like many large industries, it was often idle and even when operational it ran at well under half of capacity. What was not produced by Lever Brothers and two smaller locally-owned automated plants was made up by village soapmakers and imports. In 1975, US$367,000 worth of soap was imported, and by 1979 the amount had risen to more than US$ 2 million. These amounts were small in comparison to the import bill for raw materials for production in Ghana, as Lever Brothers, which had started life by importing thousands of tons of West African palm oil to Britain for soap production there, was now importing oil for soap production in Ghana. In 1985, the proposed import bill for commodities destined for the local soap and cosmetics industry was almost US$20 million, although probably less than half this amount was actually available. It was, in fact, the largest single item on the planned import bill for the manufacturing sector. In short,

145

soapmaking in Ghana had become a multimillion-dollar industry, and yet these figures, and the products they represent, probably served only a small portion of the Ghanaian population.

By the early 1970s, in addition to the automated plants and thousands of village soapmakers throughout the country, there were also several small urban soapmakers using basic, but essentially modern methods, and petitioning the government for import licences for caustic soda and other raw materials. In an effort to rationalize the situation, the government began to encourage the formation of co-operatives which might both increase production and pool import requirements. Possibly, it hoped as well that this might tighten quality control, for some locally produced soap was of such inferior and corrosive quality that it had earned the name 'Don't Touch Me' soap.

Soft soap

In the villages of Ghana, traditional soap is made by women from palm oil or palm kernel oil, blended with potash produced from the ashes of plantain peelings or cocoa pods. Although it has some dermatological value in treating ringworm and rashes, the soap is difficult to make, is very soft, and lasts only a few days. So the production of 'pale soap' using caustic soda instead of potash has gradually overtaken the traditional method. Whether village-made in a pot, or in town in 200-litre oil drums, 'soda soap' also had its drawbacks. The process is reasonably straightforward: palm oil is heated over a wood fire to a temperature of over 200°C in order to clarify it. It is then boiled together with caustic soda, poured into wooden moulds, and when it has cooled, is cut into bars. But because water is used as a filler, unsupervised manufacturers can reduce costs by increasing the water content above the specified maximum of 30 per cent, through the addition of more caustic soda. This does two things: it reduces the shelf life of the soap, and it can be highly detrimental to the skin, thus earning the well deserved epithet, 'Don't Touch Me'.

In the early 1970s, Lever Brothers appeared to have gone into one of its periodic declines, and soap of any kind was both hard to obtain and expensive. In 1972, a group called 'The Kumasi Soapmakers' Co-operative' approached the newly established TCC with a request for assistance in establishing a larger production unit and seeking advice on quality improvements. Before long, the Centre was drawn in. It was decided that the best way to learn the business was to start a small production facility at the TCC workshop on campus, and a prototype unit, heated electrically and capable of producing a ton of soap at a time, was set up the following year. Various combinations of palm oil, caustic soda and water were tested for hardness, colour and detergent action, and gradually, a good quality product emerged under the name 'Anchor Soap'.

By that time, the Kumasi Soapmakers' Co-operative had disintegrated into various competing family factions, but it had become evident that there were enough small-scale soap producers to justify TCC's continued involvement. In addition, the government was so encouraged by initial campus developments that it agreed in 1974 to contribute a third of the cost, in conjunction with the university and Oxfam Quebec, to the establishment of a pilot production plant away from the campus. A building was designed by the Architecture Department, constructed of soil-cement blocks, produced in block presses developed by the Department of Housing and Planning Research. When the plant opened in August 1975, it provided employment for 18 people, and seemed an ideal blend of the university's technical expertise—three departments co-operating—and of balanced financial interest and responsibility: the university, the government and an international donor.

Reducing costs

It was clear from the beginning that soapmaking could generate income for the Centre, but it was also evident that there was much research to be done on lowering costs and improving the product. One of the first problems the Centre tackled was the growing shortage of caustic soda. A lecturer in the Chemistry Department suggested that slaked lime, a waste by-product from an acetylene factory at Tema, could be used

1975: The first soapmaking plant was relatively sophisticated.

1985: Wood-fired soap boiling tanks proved more 'transferable'.

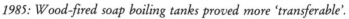

to produce caustic soda by reacting it with soda ash. Experiments were undertaken, and within a few months a small caustic soda tank had been produced which would serve as a prototype for those in most of the soapmaking plants sold by TCC over the next decade. Although the soda ash was imported, the locally produced caustic soda was roughly a quarter the cost of the imported variety, and later, the price advantage improved even more.

With assistance from ITDG and the Commonwealth Foundation, an Indian soapmaker was seconded to the Kwamo plant for three months in 1975. His first criticism was the use of electric heating elements; it was unlikely that the technology would ever extend beyond urban areas, he said, if it was dependent upon electricity. He demonstrated, in any case, that wood-fired tanks could heat the soap more quickly, were almost 75 per cent cheaper to construct, and reduced energy costs considerably. He made a number of other useful suggestions which improved the quality of the soap, and he also introduced local kaolin and cassava starch as fillers. Because inflation was beginning to affect the price of palm oil, he also suggested the use of neem oil, commonly used by village soapmakers in India, as a substitute.

In the first years there were some serious teething problems. Soda ash disappeared occasionally from the local market, necessitating imports through TCC's limited foreign exchange. Then, suddenly, between September 1974 and March 1975, Lever Brothers, long dormant, came to life again, and their 'Key' soap, similar to TCC's 'Anchor', flooded the Kumasi market. Kwamo production was maintained only by seeking markets for Anchor Soap in towns and villages beyond Kumasi. Then, as quickly as it appeared, the Lever Brothers' product disappeared, and by May 1975, the demand for Anchor soap had outstripped the capacity of the plant to produce. That month, working nights and weekends, over 12,000 bars of soap were produced, and although that rate of production would not be matched again, a respectable output of about 3,500 bars a month was maintained for the next year or so. Perhaps more important than TCC's own production was the interest shown in its process and its equipment by

149

small-scale entrepreneurs. Unlike the production of steel nuts and bolts, soapmaking was not an alien or complicated process, and the equipment was relatively inexpensive. By the end of 1975, seven small soapmaking plants had been manufactured in TCC's Plant Construction Unit, and sold to small entrepreneurs from various parts of Ghana. TCC helped to set up some of the plants, and the Kwamo factory was increasingly used for on-the-job training for workers.

Growth

By 1977, Ghana's economic decline was in full spate, and although shortages of imports tended to encourage some efforts at local import substitution, government red tape, controls, and edicts conspired to thwart many enterprises. The price of palm oil had increased by 300 per cent over the previous two years, and yet a government control price on soap meant that TCC had to sell below the cost of production. This tended not to affect small producers as much, for their products had a way of easing into the 'informal' market that was gradually encroaching on all aspects of life in Ghana. And there were things they could do to cut costs, such as increasing the water content of their soap, or reducing the size of finished bars. Neither did it affect Lever Brothers significantly, because with the cedi being exchanged at a level so unrealistic that it bordered on fantasy, their imported oil stock, when they could get it, was significantly cheaper than anything produced in Ghana.

It was the cost-price squeeze that led TCC into the de-velopment of the palm-oil press described in Chapter 8. By processing oil themselves at Kwamo, they effectively saved 50 per cent on the 1977 market price, and found that there was a demand for oil presses from other soapmakers as well. In 1977, despite the economic conditions, 20 soap-boiling tanks and associated equipment were sold to six entrepreneurs, most with caustic soda plants and most involving several weeks of training at Kwamo. That year, too, at the university's urging, the pilot plant at Kwamo was transformed into a limited company in which the university was intended to hold 55 per cent ownership, the Kwamo Village Development Committee 20 per cent, and the Kwamo Soapmakers' Association 25 per cent. Kwamotech Industries Ltd began life with a Board of Directors consisting of five university appointees but the village and the Soapmakers' Association declined to participate. With a building and equipment, considerable raw material, an import licence worth US$13,000 and the promise from government of more, it started with a reasonably good bill of health. Although it made a small loss in 1977, the previous year had seen a profit of over 13,000 cedis on a turnover of 107,000 cedis, and it was anticipated that Kwamotech had the potential to become the sort of money-spinner for the university that some had envisaged when TCC was founded.

Cost saving techniques were only a short-term solution, however, especially to the problem of oil supply. Because Ghana met only a quarter of its palm oil requirements through local production in the late 1970s, the real long-term answer was increased output. A number of ventures were encouraged at the time, both privately and through government, and by the mid-1980s, new plantations were beginning to bear fruit, with an estimated 60 per cent of palm oil consumption being met from local production. Some of this gain had been established at the expense of cocoa, however. The producer price of cocoa was so poor in 1977 that palm oil proved three times as profitable per acre, and what should have been an additional crop became in many cases an alternative. In the medium term, TCC felt that new sources of oil, particularly non-edible oils, offered a possible alternative to palm oil. Experiments were undertaken with castor, physic nut, monkey cola, and, as the expert from India had suggested, neem. But although neem had some advantages, cost was not among them, for collection from forest trees was difficult, and the establishment of a plantation would have required four or five years for the production of the first fruit. Castor oil proved most effective, but attempts to establish a commercially viable plantation at Kwamo were foiled by insect infestation and management problems.

In addition to caustic-soda production and the development of the palm-oil press, another area examined in the late 1970s was the production of perfume. Although small-scale producers were content with unperfumed soap, the addition of perfume made their product considerably more attractive when faced with competition from Lever Brothers. In 1977, TCC's Deputy Director, Ben Ntim, visited Guatemala where he happened to see a locally made steam distillation plant that could be used for perfume. Once he was back in Ghana, a copy was produced from a 200-litre oil drum attached to a long condenser fabricated at the TCC workshop. The results with lemon grass were promising, although the volumes indicated were large. If Kwamo produced a ton of soap a day, it would require 2.5 kg of perfume. The steam distiller, operating for eight hours a day, could produce 300 grams of oil from lemon grass, corresponding with about an acre of lemon grass. To service Kwamo alone, therefore, more than eight plants would be required, consuming grass from eight acres. In half a year, this could run to more than a thousand acres of lemon grass, an undertaking of such magnitude that it was better left to large-scale industry.

Slippery customers

At about this time, Lever Brothers, in search of local raw materials and other means of reducing its own import costs, approached all the universities and research institutes in Ghana for ideas. TCC provided the company with its data on lemon grass and even loaned them its distiller. It also discussed its experience with non-edible alternatives to palm oil, and, as a result, Lever Brothers queried its Indian counterpart, Hindustan Lever, on the question of neem oil. The response was not positive because of neem's hard-to-remove garlic smell, but they were positive about other TCC experiments, especially a blend of castor oil and physic nut oil. There were two results. In return for the co-operation from TCC, Lever Brothers opened its research files to TCC staff. The second was the establishment by Lever Brothers of its own castor plantation.

Meanwhile, at Kwamotech, serious management problems were developing. Although the full extent of losses through pilferage, short orders and various forms of embezzlement

152

would not become clear until an investigation was instituted in 1983, the plant's poor financial performance in the late 1970s could be explained only in part by the economic circumstances of the country. These were bad enough, however. Being a high profile, 'model' plant, Kwamotech was obliged to purchase oil from State Farms—when it was available—and at the government control price. When the official price was 875 cedis a drum in 1978, the market price was 1,600 cedis, which caused much of the official production to be siphoned into the black market, with the obvious resultant shortage at official prices. When there was no oil, Kwamotech ceased production, and even when there was, the regulation price of soap rarely covered costs. In 1973, when the project started, a drum of palm oil cost 95 cedis, but by the end of 1980, it had risen to 3,000 cedis, a thirtyonefold increase, while the control price of a bar of soap had risen less than fivefold.

The 'management problems' added to the difficulty for, in fact, a Board of Directors composed of academics resident several miles away on the UST campus was wholly inadequate for the task of serious day-to-day management, and for policing the temptations that a disintegrating economy threw so liberally in the path of a going concern with a high sales turnover and occasional access to import licences. Although TCC's involvement with Kwamotech diminished after the establishment of the company, the management lesson served to confirm what it was already learning on the light engineering side: absentee ownership and disinterested management were unlikely to work in small-scale enterprises in Ghana. And although care in the selection of clients was not the only parameter of success, without it there would be no success whatsoever.

By early 1981, TCC had sold 51 soap-boiling tanks and 11 caustic soda plants to 17 entrepreneurs across southern Ghana, as well as 50 palm-oil presses. It was a considerable achievement during such uncertain economic times. The client success rate, however, was mixed. A UST lecturer set up a small soapmaking plant with two employees near Ho, but despite considerable demand for his product, shortages of raw materials and consequent operating losses forced him out of business within

153

a year. At the same time, another client whose main activity was poultry farming, established a small TCC-built soapmaking plant after sending two men to Kwamo for training. Once established, the plant was often left to the devices of workers while the owner travelled. Productivity and quality declined. Bad soap was returned by dissatisfied customers, and eventually the owner began to operate only on advances, which were not always followed by the delivery of soap. A third customer approached TCC with an order for six soap-boiling tanks, and after considerable discussion with TCC's Peter Donkor, who also carried out a detailed feasibility study on his behalf, he obtained a bank loan for his new enterprise. Half the loan was promptly spent on a new car—not included in the feasibility study—and as a result the plant was under-capitalized and soon ran into terminal difficulties.

Several conclusions could be drawn from these and similar experiences. The most obvious are the recurring themes of client selection and management capabilities. In most societies there is a get-rich-quick mentality which can be highly detrimental to sound investment and to effective, long-term production. If it seemed more evident in Ghana than other places, it was probably a combination of a strong Ghanaian entrepreneurial streak and the opportunities—licit and illicit—created by the disasters that had befallen the economy. Because of the large demand for soap, the simplicity and low capital cost of the TCC technique, and the local availability of most of the raw materials, soapmaking could be a highly profitable enterprise in the short run, depending upon the state of play at Lever Brothers. In the case of the lecturer, his own expectations had probably been miscalculated. He could no more manage a plant and search for raw materials *in absentia* than could the Kwamotech Board of Directors. The poultry farmer seemed to have more interest in short-term profits than in the longer-term security that might have resulted from good management, and the third client placed greater priority on the purchase of a car than on his investment or his integrity.

Despite the failures, there were success stories. Grace Dansowaa Soap and Cosmetics, a small Accra toilet-soap enterprise with 13 employees, had been set up by the

154

company's namesake in 1962 and had been reasonably successful over the years. In 1975, Madame Dansowaa approached TCC for two soap-boiling tanks in order to expand into laundry soap, and over the ensuing years she managed to maintain a satisfactory level of production. Her major asset was the management experience she had gained since 1962, and her willingness to reinvest her profits in the enterprise as economic conditions changed. Two of her wisest investments were a 50 acre palm oil plantation and a small oil mill which kept her factory supplied when others went dry. Another client in Takoradi, Lovable Soap Industry, had an established relationship with the Takoradi State Farms and so had a ready source of supply that kept the firm going when others failed.

By 1984, small-scale soapmaking was a bit like a gold rush. Even Kwamotech which had still not turned a profit and had actually closed for most of 1983 while the corruption problems were sorted out, was trucking its product to the campus where bars of soap were sold on the steps of the TCC office every Friday. Some weeks the turnover exceeded 200,000 cedis (US$5,200) and market women were pleased to discover that as long as supplies held out, they could buy as much as they wanted for recycling at considerably higher prices in the market. Squabbles broke out among the academic community about allocations and entitlements. More people wanted to manufacture soap themselves. But it was a highly unstable situation, with the price of oil, 95 cedis a drum in 1973, now running somewhere between 45,000 and 60,000—when it was available.

Accounting for taste

The Government's Programme of Economic Recovery, unveiled in 1983, was soon to influence the economy of soapmaking in a variety of ways. One of the positive influences was a dramatic drop in the rate of inflation, a growth in production in almost all sectors of the economy, and a relaxation of the draconian price controls. More palm oil was soon being produced and with the *kalebule* stranglehold suddenly relaxed, the price of oil dropped to about 14,000 cedis a drum in 1985.

155

Then, without warning, Lever Brothers' products, by now almost forgotten, suddenly reappeared on the market. Although Lever Brothers still operated with imported oil and probably still had a cost advantage in raw materials despite the massive devaluations over the years, this was not the problem. Their products were, in fact, markedly more expensive than locally produced alternatives. The problem was that Ghanaians, at least a significant proportion of urbanized Ghanaians, preferred the Lever Brothers' product to the local variety. It must have been a Ghanaian economist who coined the phrase, 'There's no accounting for taste,' because in the middle of 1985, people were willing to pay twice as much for what was essentially the same product from the 'foreign' company.

On the campus, Kwamotech's weekly sales dropped to a quarter of their previous high, and TCC clients also felt the pinch. Vera Gambrah was a teacher in Kumasi who had invested in a single TCC soap-boiling tank in 1982. Despite a fire two years later, she was able to start again, and, reflecting the boom-time market, expanded to three tanks and a caustic soda plant, producing just over a ton of soap a week at the height of her production. By May 1985, everything had changed. Her production had become sporadic and she was selling off old stock at one-third of her best volume. The Lever Brothers 'Guardian' soap with which her product competed, was selling at 30 to 35 cedis a bar, while she was having difficulty getting 16 cedis for a slightly smaller bar of similar quality. Many of TCC's clients in light industry and the rural sector worried about the effects of improved production in the hitherto moribund factories of Tema and Accra, or even worse, what might happen if imports were liberalized.

There is, of course, some accounting for taste. Anybody who had lathered up once with a strong 'Don't Touch Me' soap would be happy to pay more for the assurance of quality from Lever Brothers. In this sense, Vera Gambrah and small producers like her were competing not so much against Lever Brothers, as against the fly-by-night producers who had earned local soapmaking a bad name. And regardless of the quality of Vera Gambrah's soap, her production run was so small that she was not widely known, and was unlikely ever to have adequate resources for advertising and other forms of promotion. But there was another element that was highly discouraging to small-scale enterprises that had struggled to survive through the most difficult times, producing when those with enormous resources at their command did not. It was the Ghanaian fascination with things foreign. Throughout the Third World, signs abound advertising services from tailors and doctors alike: 'Foreign Trained'. Occasionally the permutation is extended: 'Trained by Foreign Trained'. The books that have been written on this phenomenon, and who is to blame, far outweigh examples of effective solutions, although one contributing factor relates in part to Vera Gambrah's inability to advertise: it is the capacity of the large international firm to advertise, not only broadly, but using advanced techniques and sophisticated market research. Value-based advertising is especially common in soap marketing; nicely packaged toilet soap, powdered detergent and other expensive products are clearly associated more with successful, modern, upwardly mobile people, than with cleanliness. Suffice it to say that when Vera Gambrah checks the sale of soap at the corner stall just down the street from her house in Kumasi, it must hurt to find

Soap, ready for market.

157

that the 35 cedi Guardian handily outsells her own 16 cedi soap.

In fact, the truth is that there is probably boundless room for both Lever Brothers and small producers like Vera Gambrah in Ghana. The difficulty is that many of the latter have catered to a fickle urban market with discretionary spending power which allows it to make a choice when choices are available. In rural areas, there is neither the fascination with 'foreign' nor the discretionary spending power that exists in cities. At the same time as Vera Gambrah's fortunes had taken a downward turn, 16 women representing four villages were undergoing training in the TCC soapmaking method at Kwamo. They were being sponsored by the National Council on Women and Development, and were under no illusion about the cost of production and the market price of alternatives. But, in *their* villages, Lever Brothers was the figment of an elitist imagination, and even where it was not, they were not catering to the same market. Besides, no one, including Vera Gambrah, including the staff at Kwamotech and at TCC, really believed that Lever Brothers' soap would be around for long.

Despite the shakiness of local soapmaking, the cumulative effect of TCC's long effort has been positive. In addition to Kwamotech, dozens of small soapmakers are annually producing several thousand tons of good quality soap, and do so without adding to the country's foreign exchange burden. Production of soapmaking equipment has created jobs among several TCC clients in Suame who have taken over the manufacture of boiling tanks and palm-oil presses, and each soap-plant employs between three and a dozen people. Although recent comparative data are not available, 1979 figures demonstrated that capital costs of the TCC technique were extremely low. The cost per work-place for a TCC soap plant was estimated then at 3,600 cedis, which was one-tenth of the capital/labour ratio of Lever Brothers, then estimated at 36,000 cedis.[1]

Several things could happen to make soapmaking even more attractive to small producers than it has been in the past. Steady access to soda ash for the production of caustic soda would improve security for local producers. Greater amounts of palm oil are anticipated as new estates reach maturity, although only time will tell who the beneficiaries will be. Small-scale urban soap manufacturers may always have a disadvantage in competing against the more desirable Lever Brothers product when it is available, although three things might improve that situation as well. One is a method of establishing *meaningful* quality control, and therefore customer confidence in local soap. Ironically, a second would probably be a consistent level of production by Lever Brothers, rather than its long erratic absences from the market. These tend to attract local entrepreneurs to the industry and may promote a few short-term profits, but when Lever Brothers starts up again, it has the effect of damaging or destroying small-scale investment and employment, and creates a sense of wariness about small-scale productive enterprise in general.

A third factor that would help small-scale soapmakers would be the establishment of fair prices for raw materials. Although the fluctuations have been enormous over the years and may never be completely controllable, it should not be difficult for government to ensure that the cost of raw materials for local producers—soapmakers and otherwise—is not significantly undercut by import prices available to larger firms. In 1985, palm oil imports were at last banned entirely, in order to stimulate local production, although a final import of 2,700 tons was allowed in under a 1983 import licence and probably accounted for the sudden availability of Lever Brothers' soap. That shipment, at less than 10,000 cedis a drum, was perhaps the last major raw material price advantage the big manufacturer would enjoy for some time. In fact, because of the small-scale soapmakers' lower capital costs, their job creation effect, geographical spread, their import substitution value, and the comparative advantages given to large firms in the form of tax relief and repatriation of profits, a strong argument can be made for providing special arrangements and policy consider-ations for home-grown small-scale enterprises, of whom the soapmakers assisted by TCC are an excellent example.

CHAPTER 10
A Taste of Honey

Few TCC projects began because of 'somebody with a good idea'. Usually, they resulted from a combination of needs and pressures, often having their roots in the shortages and costs associated with the country's economic decline. These in turn usually had to relate in some way to existing or available TCC equipment, personnel and experience. More often than not, a new project emerged from another already underway, not as an adjunct, but as an essential component. The palm-oil press evolved from the need to reduce costs in soap production; spark plug extenders were possible because of wheel bolt production, and wheel bolts were being made because years before, truck-body makers in Suame had required coach bolts. Foundry work evolved out of experience with traditional brass-casters and the growing awareness that the source of scrap steel was finite. Although many beekeeping projects around the world have undoubtedly resulted from the idea that honey production might be a good income generator, that is not how it happened at TCC.

In 1975, when TCC began to work with the traditional brass-casters at Kurofofurom, there was a shortage of almost all the raw materials they needed, including the beeswax they used in the lost wax method of casting. Ironically, it was the lost wax method of casting bronze that had encouraged beekeeping in ancient Egypt, although honey was, in itself, so highly thought of in early Mediterranean societies that Alexander the Great was buried in it. In Ghana, too, honey has always been highly regarded, as a sweetener and for medicinal purposes. But beekeeping was not widely known. Honey was gathered by individuals, usually men, who were sometimes known as 'bee killers'. They sought out wild hives in the forest, and simply smoked or burned the bees out, often cutting the

160

tree down in the process. Some individuals were known as 'bee havers' instead of bee killers, because they were fortunate enough to own a tree in which bees nested, and in the north there were some people who baited up-ended clay pots, encouraged hives, and then smoked the bees out when they were ready to harvest. Generally speaking, however, 'bee killing' was the norm. The result, a dirty honey that often contained bits of dead bees and tasted of smoke, was nevertheless highly sought after, and financially was well worth the trouble of getting it. The beeswax, however, except around villages like Kurofofurom, was simply discarded once the honey had been squeezed out of it. It was this discarded beeswax that TCC was originally interested in.

The Kenyan connection

Through the Commonwealth Secretariat, TCC made contact with professional East African beekeepers, and in 1979, using diagrams received from Kenya, three models of the Kenya top-bar hive were constructed. By chance, the day the three were completed and delivered to the TCC office, a representative of an American NGO arrived to ask if TCC had any information that might assist them in a beekeeping project they were starting in Brong Ahafo. Two of the three hives departed with the visitor, who turned out to be the first of hundreds, and the third was set up at the UST Botanical Garden. It did not take long for the first hive and the next two to be colonized, but after that the Centre was at something of a loss as to what to do. Further correspondence with the Commonwealth Secretariat finally resulted in financial assistance for a month-long trip to East Africa. Two people went; a representative from the Forest Products Research Institute, and Kwesi Opoku-Debrah from TCC. The visit to Kenya and Tanzania opened a new panorama of ideas. Both countries had developed respectable export industries in honey, and it was discovered that beeswax had an almost limitless range of applications in industry, textiles, cleaning and polishing materials, in pharmaceuticals, dental work, adhesives, food, paper and ink production and in preservatives.

161

Quite apart from the potential export market for honey, there already existed a ready local market beyond that served by traditional honey gatherers. In 1975 Ghana imported more than US$17 million worth of sugar, and the following year the amount rose to over $23 million. Although it had dropped considerably by 1979, the reduction reflected more the shortage of foreign exchange than increased local production or slackening of demand. Without doubt, if beekeeping could be developed, it offered limitless possibilities.

Not long after Kwesi Opoku-Debrah returned to Ghana with sample veils, bee suits, smokers and other beekeeping equipment, he became involved in the minimum tillage farm project, and gradually beekeeping fell to Stephen Adjare. Adjare had come to TCC under the National Service Scheme as a weaver, but as thread disappeared from the market, TCC's broadloom project fell into abeyance. Adjare had followed the beekeeping discussions since his arrival at TCC in 1976, and when he discovered that the first TCC hive at the Botanical Garden had been colonized, he decided to buy one for himself. He hung it under a tree near his house and 28 days later it was colonized. Adjare was stung, not by the bees, but by the idea, and he spent weeks poring over all the literature he could find in the UST library, visiting other institutions and government departments and persuading friends to buy hives for themselves. They could not lose; a single hive could more than pay for itself in the first year.

So infectious was his excitement and enthusiasm, that TCC organized a national workshop on beekeeping in January 1981, which was attended by 53 delegates from across Ghana. It was opened by the Deputy Minister of Agriculture who encouraged delegates to make recommendations to government on ways an industry might be encouraged, and much favourable publicity was generated. A National Beekeepers' Association was one of the outcomes of the conference, and because some of the participants were Peace Corps Volunteers, they took the idea away with them to their postings. It was also discovered that Stephen Adjare had the special talent of holding an audience spellbound with his enthusiasm for bees. Soon requests began to arrive for more information, for hives, and for training.

162

Like so many technologies, beekeeping is deceptively simple. The Kenya top-bar hive is a simple coffin-shaped box, 97 cm in length, 28 cm high, 30.5 cm wide at the bottom, and 56 cm at the top. A series of 27 wedge-shaped wooden bars fit snugly across the top, and a lid is placed over that. Although a good carpenter can easily copy the hive, it is essential that the dimensions of the 'top bars' are followed precisely. Their width, 3.2 cm, has been scientifically determined in order to allow enough space for the manoeuvrability of bees between the combs that will eventually form on the bars. Ten small entrance holes are cut into the base of the hive, smeared with bait (beeswax is ideal) and with luck, the hive will soon be colonized.

Depending on the location of the hive and the time of year, this can take anywhere from a few days to three months. However, it was soon discovered that, except in the heavy forests of south-western Ghana, there was nowhere that bees did not thrive. During the swarming season, a single colony could produce ten or more swarms, and although only a few thousand bees might enter the hive, the population would expand to 50,000 or more at full maturity. Starting at one end of the hive or the other, the bees soon begin producing combs which hang down separately from each top bar. At harvest time, with the aid of a smoker to drive bees away from the outside of the hive, the top is lifted. Again using the smoker, the bees are driven back into the occupied portion of the hive. The first bar with a comb attached is then lifted out, trimmed and replaced, and the process is repeated with each bar until the hive has been harvested. After the combs are squeezed and the resulting honey is strained, it is ready for consumption.

The Ghanaian honey bee turned out to be an excellent forager, thriving equally on neem, acacia, coconut, mango and other fruit trees, and anything else that flowered, and early yields turned out to be significantly higher than yields in Kenya and Tanzania. Start-up equipment was minimal. Although professional beekeepers in Europe and North America work with a variety of paraphernalia, the most essential equipment apart from the hive is the smoker, gloves, a hat and veil. The first smokers were made by a tinsmith at Kwamo using old tin

163

cans and inner tube rubber for the bellows, although later a larger, more durable model was manufactured in Suame. Locally made straw hats with mosquito netting and a drawstring were a simple enough affair, and gloves could either be purchased in the market or produced by tailors from locally available cloth. There were other desirable items such as a TCC-designed 'bee suit', but it required six yards of cloth, and by 1980, this was beyond the means of the average Ghanaian.

In January 1981, the basic kit—hive, veil, gloves and smoker—was available from TCC for 455 cedis, and despite inflation, there had only been a 95 cedi increase 18 months later. If a hive yielded 40 kg of honey in a year, at the 1982 Kumasi price of roughly 80 cedis per kg, the gross income would exceed 3,000 cedis, and there would be a clear profit of almost 2,500 cedis in the first year. Although by then the exchange rate was meaningless, as a point of comparison 2,500 cedis officially represented over US$900. Even if the yield was half that amount, the return on the investment was still excellent. The public response was also excellent. The demand for workshops and demonstration sessions increased rapidly, especially after TCC's joint 'Ghana Can Make It' Exhibition in Accra with the Clients' Association. Top-bar hives were turned out by the dozen for clients small and large. The Ghana Beekeepers' Association began to hold regular meetings, and TCC started publishing a quarterly journal called *The Ghana Bee News*, full of useful hints, technical data and news of membership activity.

The sting

Of course, no enterprise is as simple, as straightforward and as profitable as the picture painted so far. African bees are not nearly as docile as those found in Europe and North America. They do not respond nearly as well to management—pest control, pruning, thinning, harvesting and prevention of swarming. They are more likely to sting than other bees, and the TCC experience is replete with examples. The most dramatic took place during the first National Workshop in 1981 when Stephen Adjare held a succulent honeycomb

164

Stephen Adjare's enthusiasm for bees rarely resulted in stings.

triumphantly aloft for the benefit of a throng of participants who had gone to the Botanical Garden for a 'practical'. The bees took umbrage and swarmed over delegates, dignitaries and innocent passers-by, stinging all profusely. As TCC Director John Powell put it; 'The unprotected spectators had been advised that in such an event they should beat a slow and dignified retreat. Some succeeded in retaining a modicum of dignity. Many did not. Some abandoned a vertical orientation and rolled about on the grass and under bushes . . .'[1] It was, of course, no laughing matter; even experienced beekeepers are stung from time to time, and can eventually develop a toxic reaction that affects the whole body. One young Peace Corps Volunteer who attempted in vain to save some chickens and goats that were under attack, received 50 stings himself and then went into shock, which eventually led to a partially collapsed lung and pneumonia. In contrast, however, a Ghanaian colleague, stung more than 300 times on the same occasion, suffered only localized surface discomfort.

The bees also suffer discomfort and are subject to disease, invasion by ants, wax moths and other insects. They are also a favourite meal of lizards and certain birds. If there is too much annoyance, which can include children, goats rubbing against the stand or curious adults, they may suddenly 'abscond'. Or they may simply abscond out of perverse volition. Slash-and-burn farming is another serious detriment to beekeeping. And there are unforeseen hazards with a peculiarly Ghanaian flavour. One farmer at Ayikuma in the Shai Hills, for example, visited the five hives he had purchased from TCC and found them all individually burned to ashes. A subsequent investigation revealed that he had inadvertently placed them on a former burial ground over which there was an unresolved land dispute between five chiefs. Seeing the hives, people thought they were *juju*—small coffins, one representing each chief—and burned them. In the *Ghana Bee News*, Stephen Adjare reported the incident under the headline, '150,000 Industrious Workers Burned to Death'.[2]

Hives of activity

Nevertheless, despite the difficulties, demand for hives and equipment flourished. The National Service Secretariat placed large orders and had the TCC conduct workshops for many of its young graduates. The Peace Corps continued to disseminate information through TCC workshops. Local groups and organizations ordered hives, sometimes singly or in pairs, sometimes by the dozen. The Akuapem Rural Development Foundation ordered 50, and by mid-1985, an estimated 1,500 hives had been sold through TCC or TCC clients. Probably many more had been copied privately. Reported yields varied

Table 5: Economic Return on Beekeeping

IN KUMASI	Year 1	Year 2
Kenya top-bar hive	¢ 2,000	–
Smoker	575	–
Veil	650	–
Gloves	300	–
Total cost	¢ 3,525	–
Income: 20 kg at ¢ 200	4,000	¢ 4,000
Net profit	¢ 475	¢ 4,000

IN TAMALE	Year 1	Year 2
Kenya top-bar hive	¢ 1,500	–
Smoker	300	–
Veil	250	–
Gloves	300	–
Total cost	¢ 2,350	–
Income: 15 kg at ¢ 200	3,000	¢ 3,000
Net profit	¢ 650	¢ 3,000

dramatically, although this probably reflected mixed management practices more than anything else. Reports from the most favourable geographic areas indicated yields of 20 kg per hive over a six-month period; in the humid rain forest, there were yields between 20 and 30 kg annually, and on the dry Accra Plain there were equally good yields. Tentative results from the north showed harvests of 23 to 32 kg a year.

Taking a conservative average of 20 kg per hive in the Kumasi area and 15 kg in Tamale, which allows latitude for failure and absconding, the 1985 profitability picture was as shown in Table 5.

What these figures indicate is that, in actual fact, there was probably a fairly small return on beekeeping in the first year of operation, perhaps enough to purchase a dozen loaves of bread. Considering the labour involved in obtaining and establishing a hive, the care and maintenance and other incidental costs such as bottles, transportation and so on, the actual profit in the first year is probably closer to zero; and with a single hive, everything could be lost if the bees absconded. In order to reduce the risk, a minimum of two hives is almost essential, although this doubles the capital investment. It is only in the second year and beyond (the hives have a life expectancy of five years or more, depending on care and maintenance), that the real income begins to flow.

There is another potential source of income, however, which was the original impetus for the project: beeswax. Although TCC's work with the brass-casters had ceased, a number of immediate uses for wax suggested themselves. TCC experiments had shown that it made an excellent wood preservative, and in the north, the National Council on Women and Development, the Christian Mothers' Association and others regarded wax as a raw material for use in women's projects. It made a clean, sweet-smelling candle in areas where kerosene was expensive or non-existent, for example; but there was an even greater potential. The industrial value of beeswax on the world market is considerable; roughly half is used in the manufacture of cosmetics, about 25 to 30 per cent in pharmaceuticals and the balance in dentistry, lithography, engraving, polishes and church candles. In 1982, an Accra manufacturing concern that was importing beeswax from Europe wrote to TCC saying that it would be interested in discussing the purchase of 20 tons, which at the time had a value of more than £46,000, before freight, duties and taxes. Of course the enquiry was premature, as almost no beeswax was yet being collected, and the volumes indicated were large. Generally, the yield of wax to honey is in the ratio of about 1:15. At 20 kg of honey annually per hive, an estimated 15,000 hives would be required for the supply of 20 tons of beeswax, and this assumes an efficient collection network and refining capacity.

Although the task appeared daunting, the sale of 1,500 hives in four years was not an insignificant beginning, and the collection of beeswax was not a difficult proposition. Wax is sometimes obtained by boiling. After the honey has been squeezed out, the comb is tied in a piece of cloth and placed in boiling water. The wax melts, seeps through the cloth leaving the detritus behind, and can then be skimmed from the top of the water. It is a dangerous practice, however, for the wax is highly volatile in this state, and can explode. As an alternative, TCC developed a simple little wooden solar extractor, essentially a box with a sheet of polyethylene covering it, which is clean, efficient, safe and inexpensive.

Is there honey still for tea?

TCC encouraged beekeepers to take their beeswax to central buying centres—an agency was established, for example, near the Kumasi Lorry Park. But initial progress was slow. One of the problems was publicity, another finance. The entire beekeeping project had operated from the beginning on a shoestring, funded largely from TCC's own recurring budget and a few very small grants from interested parties. The International Bee Research Association, for example, provided several hundred dollars worth of literature, and Johnson's Wax (Ghana) Ltd, not itself a consumer of beeswax, donated 10,000 cedis in 1983. The project had benefited greatly from the assignment of several Peace Corps volunteers in its first years, but even so, it was understaffed and its mobility was severely restricted. Nevertheless, the progress was impressive.

169

Stephen Adjare, originally a weaver, had become Ghana's best known and best liked beekeeper, and in a few short years, had become the country's foremost authority on the subject. In 1983, ITDG published his book, *The Golden Insect: A Handbook on Beekeeping for Beginners*. The first thousand copies were shipped to Ghana and sold out almost overnight, necessitating a second printing of five thousand. But Adjare knew as well as anyone that there was much work to do. Because of his limited mobility and the tiny size of the unit, he had concentrated early efforts on Kumasi and Accra, and apart from some of the institutional customers, many of the individual beekeepers were educated, urban people—teachers, retired civil servants, small-scale businessmen. In an effort to spread the technology to rural areas, greater efforts were made after 1983 to hold workshops in smaller towns and villages, taking TCC to the country rather than waiting for villagers to come to Kumasi.

Follow-up training and advice was also important, for despite initial workshop enthusiasm, many people were still afraid of the bees, and once hives were installed, many avoided them, ignoring the lessons of hive management at the expense of their yield. These people had reverted, in fact, to the level of 'bee haver'. Another possibility was the introduction of cost saving techniques in order to make the first year more attractive financially. One idea was a modification of the traditional beekeeping technique used in the north. There, some people kept bees in large overturned clay pots. A baited hole at the base attracted the bees, and when the time came to harvest, the bees were simply smoked or burned out. A more lasting and productive variation being attempted in 1985 was the use of Kenya-style top bars on the traditional pot, a blend of the old and the more scientific approach. TCC anticipated that beekeeping would eventually have great appeal in the north, and with the completion of the Tamale ITTU, a full-time beekeeping co-ordinator was assigned there in 1985. A promising development for the use of honey in the north had come about through UNICEF's oral rehydration programme which stressed the use of sugar—often not available, and very expensive when it was. Honey was an ideal local substitute.

And there was still much research to be done on the Ghanaian bee, of which there are many varieties. Some of the best foragers are also the most aggressive, and they respond poorly to management. In 1985, Stephen Adjare took a sabbatical leave from TCC to study queen rearing in the United States. It was hoped that one possibility might be to breed a more docile bee among the good foragers. Another aim was to find ways of speeding up the colonization of hives. Rather than leave colonization to time and chance, hives could be colonized quickly, or recolonized easily in the case of abandonment, through a programme of queen rearing and nucleus colony development at TCC. If this could be done, many more skeptics and small farmers might be drawn in.

Some of these ideas are for the future, but a solid foundation has been laid for a programme which has demonstrated great potential as an income-earning activity, for women as well as men, for farmers and for people with little or no land. Beekeeping has already established its import substitution value, and its potential in the related activities and industries which benefit from honey and beeswax. The success so far has a great deal to do with an existing demand for honey, both in itself and as a substitute for sugar. The project has benefited from the fact that it can provide a reasonable return on investment and personal labour without a great deal of dependence on external support, marketing systems or technical expertise. Everything involved is entirely local. And the capital outlay is small enough that the technology is within the means of the average Ghanaian family, if not through savings then through a co-operative or on hire-purchase. And although good yields require good management, ultimately it is the bees that provide the labour.

CHAPTER 11
Tamale and Beyond

Some appropriate technology institutions are geographically restricted in scope; they tend to focus on their own immediate environment, and fail to spread their knowledge beyond the confines of a one or two hour drive from where they are located. This has not been the case with TCC, which worked hard over its first dozen years to provide a national service within Ghana, especially in the north. Without assistance from USAID, the Tamale Intermediate Technology Transfer Unit would probably never have existed, although the saga of its establishment, outlined in Chapter 6, hardly reflected the original plan put forward by TCC in 1975.

In its Fourth Annual Review, TCC stated that,

'. . . as the only technological university in Ghana, the University of Science and Technology must play a national role. During its first four years of activity, the Technology Consultancy Centre operated only one office on the university campus at Kumasi, and although it executed projects at locations remote from Kumasi, it was effective in depth only in the Ashanti Region. To build a truly national capability will require additional bases of operation . . .'

The idea coincided with the government's aim to expand and improve the quality of education in the north. There was no institution of higher education north of Kumasi, not even a polytechnic, and when the University of Science and Technology was asked to look into the feasibility of establishing a northern campus, TCC was a part of the investigating committee. Although bilateral donors began taking an interest in appropriate technology around that time, it was not until 1979 that USAID actually signed an agreement with the Government of Ghana to cover the construction and equipping of a Tamale ITTU, and by that time the idea of a 'northern campus' had

172

been placed in abeyance. It was a full six years after signing the infamous agreement that the building specified in it was actually erected. In some ways, however, the delay was fortuitous, for it allowed TCC time—much more than it would have liked, no doubt—to become familiar with the Northern Region, and to mature in its approach to clients and product development in the south.

Some of TCC's earliest projects had their roots in the north. The first broadlooms developed and manufactured at TCC were sent to mission schools in Nandom and other northern towns. The first involvement with animal traction—bullock ploughs, wagons and spare parts—was centred in the Northern and Upper Regions. And the pedal rice-thresher was developed for eventual use in the north. The north was, however, fundamentally different from the south, in climate, ethnic and religious make-up, and in the pace of development. Like the railway, much stopped at Kumasi. Roads were poor, health services were underdeveloped, and the educational infrastructure was stunted. Small villages were dotted sparsely across vast areas of dry savannah; only recently did the population of the entire Northern Region, the largest in the country, grow to more than a million. Although efforts had been made to introduce large-scale rice farming, the essential characteristics of agriculture were much as they had been for generations—shifting cultivation managed largely by hoe, cutlass and sweat. Formal credit institutions were few and far between, and government extension services were sparse. Trading, especially on the part of market women, was not as widespread as in the south, and technology had not yet reached the stage where equipment, even simple equipment, could be manufactured according to scientific design. In itself, this was not an entirely bad thing, for ignorance of the modern sector meant that villages in the north were often more self reliant than in the south, and age-old technologies had in some cases managed to survive.

When Frank Robertson made a survey of the north, he found that the less accessible a village was to cars and trucks, the less likely it was to have a serious food shortage. People did not rely on outside inputs for agriculture, and they tended to

173

have more efficient, long-term storage techniques against localized shortages and poor harvests. And he discovered village blacksmiths smelting iron and producing agricultural implements, much as they and their predecessors had probably done for centuries.

So, as plans for the Tamale ITTU were adjusted and re-adjusted to suit the time constraints imposed by the funding agency, so was the idea that Tamale could be a copy of the Kumasi experience. For one thing, there was nothing in Tamale that resembled Suame Magazine, and only a few small machine shops existed with anything like the potential that existed in Kumasi. One of them was run by a man named Alhaji Issa Goodman, who had started as a blacksmith and keymaker in 1975. When TCC discovered Alhaji Goodman in 1978, he had a competent little workshop which produced metal water-tanks and boxes, and repaired or modified imported bullock ploughs. A great many German mould-board ploughs had been imported into Ghana, and because northern farmers preferred the ridger plough with two shares, Goodman had found a market in adapting them. A TCC technician was sent to Tamale to work with Goodman on welding and other techniques, and in a few months, a number of improvements had been introduced. Goodman's welders, for example, had been using a slow, double welding technique, but with a little training, they reduced the time involved by two-thirds, and were producing a better, cheaper water tank. As with some Kumasi artisans, Goodman's son was sent to the Suame ITTU for training on a centre lathe and in welding, and later TCC assisted in obtaining a few small pieces of machinery and some tooling for the shop in Tamale.

Spinning ladies

As progress on the USAID project lurched forward, some pieces began to fall into place, albeit places which had not been part of the original scheme. Machine tools started to arrive in Ghana before the prefabricated building, and an effort was made to find alternative locations for them. Some were stored in Kumasi; a capstan lathe was loaned to Alhaji Goodman. At one stage, when TCC had almost despaired of the USAID building, it was thought that perhaps the ITTU could be located at the Technical Institute, upgraded in 1984 to a Polytechnic, where other machine tools were being stored. One result of that idea was a plan for the ITTU to operate in close conjunction with the school, offering classes and workshops for its students, and apprenticeships for its graduates. Frank Robertson moved to Tamale in 1983 to become TCC's first resident representative in the north, and he spent much of his first year cataloguing resources and raw materials, identifying skills and technologies, as well as individuals who might share a common interest with each other and with TCC. He established an 'Appropriate Technology Club' which he operated out of his home, setting up a workshop with a generator and some small machine tools in his garage.

Within a year he had more than a hundred members; a core group of 16, under the patronage of Alhaji Issa Goodman, began to discuss the idea of working together in a centralized location. Eventually, six acres of land were obtained not far from the ITTU site, while training and product development continued at Robertson's house. One member of the group was a welder, another was a carpenter, a third had a crude aluminium foundry, and among the others were an electrician, a potter and a mason. Together, it was anticipated that they could offer each other services and assistance, and with help from TCC, perhaps form the nucleus of a small-scale informal industrial centre—with any luck, one that was less chaotic then Suame Magazine.

One group that had taken an early interest in the Appropriate Technology Club was a number of women who earned extra income in their spare time by spinning cotton. The technique was time consuming and laborious, and as a result, younger women had lost interest in it, especially during the days when cheap cotton garments had flooded out of southern textile mills. Because TCC's own work in weaving had ceased due to shortages of cotton yarn, the women sparked an early and enthusiastic interest in spinning, and work began on developing a spinning wheel which might speed up their production. After

175

The traditional method of spinning cotton is time consuming.

The TCC spinning wheel is cheap and infinitely faster.

three prototypes, a suitable model was developed which minimized the use of wood, had a crank-shaft of mild steel rod, used a small amount of cord and a bobbin made from an old tin can. The new wheel cut production time, resulted in a stronger yarn, and the 'spinning ladies', as they became known, pronounced themselves satisfied and impressed with the development.

By that time, the ITTU building had at last been erected, and the equipment that had been scattered in various places around Tamale and in Kumasi was gradually being assembled. It was planned that the first workshop to be established at the ITTU would be for woodworking, and the second would probably be a foundry. Among the initial products would be spinning wheels for the ladies which, combined with a study of their productivity and profitability, might indicate the potential for a more widespread cottage spinning industry. A second product would be the Kenya top-bar beehive, already in considerable demand since the posting to Tamale earlier in 1985 of a full-time Beekeeping Co-ordinator. And it was likely that with the return of cotton yarn to the market-place, some of the schools that were training girls in the art of weaving would require additional looms. A more ambitious but important additional possibility for the woodwork shop was pattern making for foundry work, especially because of an abundance in the north of highly suitable softwoods.

Now that an ITTU has been established in Tamale, its *modus operandi* will require development, and it will probably take some years, as it did in the south, before the ultimate direction has been worked out. Because the level of technology in northern Ghana's rural industries is appreciably different from what pertains in the south, client development, product mix and speed of progress will likely all be different. There will not be as much demand for machine tools as in the south, and so for some years, concentration is likely to be on hand tools. There is not the abundance of scrap in Tamale that Kumasi enjoys, and so products will have to be developed which take into consideration the availability of different raw materials. Because the north is much closer to farming, agricultural projects and products will most likely dominate TCC work in

177

Tamale. Electricity is erratic there, and the availability of diesel fuel has been unreliable. This will undoubtedly mean less emphasis on motor driven products such as the corn-milling machine or the cassava grater which have become commonplace in the south. Human-powered machines such as the pedal-driven rice thresher will be the focus of early attention. And a *modus vivendi* will have to be worked out with Kumasi; in the early stages of development at Tamale, a close relationship is highly desirable, but in time, a certain amount of decentralization and independence will be necessary. In short, there is much to be done in Tamale. But perhaps because of the delays, a more solid relationship with individuals, local government, educational institutions and small-scale enterprises has been established than might have been the case had the USAID project gone ahead as planned.

The international connection

Given the level of activity at TCC and the discussion in Chapter 6 of its experience with bilateral aid agencies, it might be assumed that TCC has operated on large budgets, heavily funded by external agencies. This is, in fact, not the case. In 1983, for example, the total combined income for both TCC and the Suame ITTU was approximately 1.8 million cedis. At the exchange rate prevailing in January of that year, this would have been approximately US$650,000, although with devaluations, by the end of 1983 it had an official value of less than $51,000. Although US$250,000 worth of external assistance arrived in that year, most of it was in the form of residual equipment and vehicles from the old CIDA and USAID projects. At Suame, on sales of 816,000 cedis, a profit of 400,000 cedis was realized on the manufacturing account, providing a net excess of income over expenditure of roughly 100,000 cedis. Of the total income in 1983, 37 per cent had been earned through the manufacture and sale of industrial products and equipment, a level of earnings that had held constant over the previous decade.

Apart from the financial support provided by external agencies, a broader dimension to the Centre's international

178

relationships developed over the years. It had two aspects, the first of which was the learning experience gained through contact with other AT institutions. The second was what TCC could teach, both to other AT institutions and to groups interested in learning from a particular Ghanaian experience. When TCC began in 1972, appropriate technology as a discipline was still in its infancy. *Small is Beautiful* had not yet been published, and although organizations such as ITDG were actively fostering the concept, the number of Third World institutions for whom it was a prime focus was small. By 1977, however, the movement had blossomed, and more than 500 AT institutions existed world-wide. By 1980, the number had soared to an estimated 1,000.

While it may have seemed in the late 1970s that appropriate technology was an idea whose time had come, the proliferation of organizations was a difficult phenomenon to assess. Many were small, one-off groups without a clear rationale; some were collections of hobbyists, while others were more traditional organizations with new labels to reflect changing trends in development and donor attitudes. Bold claims were frequently made in development literature about new breakthroughs, revolutionary concepts and other marvels of appropriate technology that were going to fundamentally and rapidly alter the face of Third World society. In a 1982 ITDG assessment, however, the conclusions were mixed. While it was clear that appropriate technology had been popularized and accepted as a viable concept, solid progress in its application was more difficult to demonstrate. 'Examples of projects which have taken technologies beyond the pilot stage into widespread production and use are very thin on the ground. This remains the case, moreover, even after considerable support given to the AT movement over the past five years by governments and international agencies.'[1]

For an organization like TCC, attempting to find inter-national partners whose experience was similar or relevant was not easy. In the Third World, AT institutions could be divided into three categories. The first were those connected either directly or indirectly to government, such as the Botswana Technology Centre, the South Pacific Appropriate Technology

179

Foundation in Papua New Guinea, or Tanzania's Arusha Appropriate Technology Project. The second group consisted of those which fell under the category of academic or research institutions, focusing especially on appropriate technology. Some of these, like TCC, were also indirectly linked to government through funding and other relationships. The Small Industry Research, Training and Development Organization in India, the Development Technology Centre at the Bandung Institute of Technology, and the Advisory Services Unit for Technology Research and Development at the University of Sierra Leone were examples. The third category consisted of non-governmental organizations which proliferated in number after the mid-1970s, with almost as many closing down as opened. CEMAT, the Centro de Estudios Meso-americanos y de Technologia Apropida in Guatemala, was one of the larger, more consistently successful appropriate technology NGOs, while the Appropriate Technology Development Association (ATDA) in India was an example of an organization that began under the aegis of an academic body, and broke away to become an NGO.

Some of TCC's ideas, motivation and encouragement came from these institutions and others. The steam distillation plant developed for perfume extraction at TCC was modelled on a successful device that Deputy Director Ben Ntim had seen when he visited CEMAT in Guatemala. TCC's palm-oil press was copied from a Sierra Leonean model. The Kenya top-bar beehive was brought back from East Africa after a trip there by Kwesi Opoku-Debrah. Minimum tillage farming was learned from the International Institute for Tropical Agriculture in Nigeria. The most significant developments in TCC's soap-making came about as a result of innovations introduced by a soapmaker sent from India by ATDA to work with TCC. And the pedal rice-thresher was gradually improved after various TCC technicians studied Philippine models and techniques at the International Rice Research Institute.

TCC staff travelled widely over the years, and their work enjoyed the benefit of regular contact with the international academic university network, as well as with the appropriate technology network. On the academic side, TCC was asked to

180

advise on the establishment of TCC-style university-based institutions in Kenya, Zambia, Papua New Guinea, Fiji and Nepal, as well as on possibilities for First World universities to become involved in AT outreach into the Third World. On the appropriate technology side, special training programmes were organized in Britain, the USA, India and other countries in basics such as foundry work or lathe operation, as well as in more esoteric subjects like queen-bee breeding. UNESCO, IDRC, CIDA, USAID, ITDG and other international funding agencies were helpful in fostering this sort of sabbatical or on-the-job training. Probably the most important connection for TCC has been with India and the Appropriate Technology Development Association in Lucknow. TCC's Director, John Powell, spent several months there in 1977 as a visiting professor while on sabbatical, and was so impressed that TCC subsequently published a booklet on ATDA, aimed at stimulating thinking on appropriate technology in Ghana. Since then, several senior TCC staff have visited ATDA to work on specific projects and to absorb some of the ambience and inspiration that make India both a spiritual and a practical centre of appropriate technology.

The international experience has not all been one way, however. Travelling TCC staff have undoubtedly left their mark behind, even while on training programmes. Visitors on their own study programmes have travelled to Kumasi from places as far apart and as diverse as Lusaka and Lae, while TCC has been invited to deliver papers or participate in conferences from Mexico to Melbourne. To a certain extent, however, the lasting effect of conferences, especially conferences on a subject as location- and culture-specific as appropriate tech-nology, have a nebulous impact. More solid, in TCC's experience, are the actual development projects carried out in other countries by its workers. Stephen Adjare, for example, assisted in the establishment of beekeeping projects in Nigeria and Togo, spreading what TCC had learned with the Kenya top-bar hive beyond Ghana. And Peter Donkor undertook several training missions around Africa to help establish small soapmaking plants.

One of the first such missions took place in 1978 when

181

Service Quaker asked if TCC could help establish soapmaking plants in Guinea-Bissau. After a two-week familiarization trip to the country, Peter Donkor returned to Ghana to organize a training programme at TCC, and subsequently six men and women representing three different groups in Guinea-Bissau arrived for a ten-week course which culminated in the production of their own personal batches of soap at Kwamo. A second project was undertaken the following year to train members of a women's co-operative in Mali, and in 1980 a rural soapmaking plant was established in Sierra Leone as an income generation project for a rural health organization. Subsequent projects were successfully undertaken in neighbouring Togo and, at the opposite end of the continent, in Mozambique.

The travel and the international outreach, almost all of which was funded by external development agencies, has been important to TCC in several ways. It undoubtedly contributed to the development of a basic staff commitment to the concept of appropriate technology. Through Ghana's darkest days, through the terrible austerity, the red tape and the *kalebule*, they found the inspiration they needed in order to stay with projects, not only through their day-to-day work, but through the community of interest they found internationally, whether it was in the villages of India or the research institutes of the West. And certainly there was learning. New ideas, whether small adjustments to an existing technique or an entirely new approach to a problem, whether accidental or carefully planned, returned to Ghana with the travellers. More valuable than technologies or techniques, however, was what TCC workers learned about how a successful transfer had taken place in another society.

All of this was important, and it helped reinforce TCC's philosophy about re-inventing the wheel. The most successful ideas that came back with the travellers were those that were logical successors to existing projects, technologies or methodologies. And the most successful export—soapmaking—was effective in other African countries for the same reason it had been successful in Ghana. A market existed, the technology was based on locally available raw materials and equipment, and the method was not significantly more complicated than well known traditional techniques. In TCC's experience, it was not necessary to re-invent the wheel, but it was absolutely essential that societies, and groups within them, appreciate and thoroughly absorb new technologies into their own framework of the world. The *Twi* proverb, 'Little by little the chicken drinks water', was relevant; an industrial revolution could proceed quickly; but without an orderly progression, without a collective experience of its various stages, it would be unlikely to succeed.

CHAPTER 12

No Condition Permanent

The appropriate technology movement emerged from the debate about the great technology gap that exists between Third World and industrialized nations, about the whys and hows of reducing the gap, and about the most effective means of 'transferring technology'. In over four centuries of contact between 'Europeans' and what came to be known as the 'Third World', technology has not so much been 'transferred' as sold. In the second half of this century, it has been sold through turnkey operations, development assistance programmes and foreign investment; it has been sold by multinational corporations, aid agencies and travelling salesmen, to governments, entrepreneurs and co-operatives. Whatever the mechanism, there has usually been a customer and a payment. In Ghana's case, much of it was paid for by the cocoa farmer, who received little thanks or recompense. It was the difference between what cocoa realized on the world market and what was paid to the producer that financed the exchequer for years and paid for Ghana's huge, unrequited investment in industry, a trickle-down—or perhaps a 'trickle-up'—approach to fiscal policy that worked admirably, for a while. The price of technology has been steep, not only because the terms of trade between those with the technology and those without has been bad (and getting worse), but because the technology itself has often borne little relevance to the conditions in, and needs of the countries in which it was supposed to work.

Choice of technology

'Appropriate' technology was the logical recourse. The literature on intermediate and appropriate technology, however, rings with the anguish of those who have seen good idea

184

after good idea end up rusting outside the workshop of a research and development institution. Although by no means as dramatic or as expensive as a capital-intensive tyre factory working at a fraction of capacity, the large plywood grain-storage silo (developed by professors at UST) that required a motorized drier and had to be kept indoors for fear of rain, was a manifestation of the same problem. In the case of the tyre factory—and there is such an example in Ghana—problems of raw materials, management, foreign exchange, and maintenance all took their toll. The particular tragedy of the tyre plant is that its productivity was so low, its plant so run-down, its prospects so poor, that when money became available for reconstruction of the Ghanaian economy in the early 1980s, it made more sense to import tyres than to use the funds to paper over the factory's problems.

With hindsight, it is easy enough to say that before the investment was made, these things should have been considered. But the 'appropriate' grain storage silo which sits unused under a thatch shelter on a farm near Kumasi is not very different. At the time, it *seemed* appropriate, it seemed as though it would work, it seemed to solve a straightforward problem, just as the tyre factory no doubt did to those who made the original investment. The difference between the two cases, apart from the fact that the grain storage silo is idle while the tyre factory still produces a few tyres—probably at a negative value added and a heavy cost in foreign exchange—is that when the original decisions were made, the choices in one case were more limited than in the other. Modern tyre manufacturing equipment is not widely available, and cannot be readily adapted to suit special conditions of management, climate, material supply and so on. The capital intensity and complexity of the plant cannot be altered to suit the specific skill and labour mix of an individual customer. If you are going to start producing your own tyres, sooner or later 'you pays your money and you takes your chances'. (The fact that something like 2 per cent of the world's research and development expenditure is devoted to the particular needs of the Third World helps explain why the choices are so limited, but that is another story.) In the case of the grain storage silo, however, many choices were available, and yet the same sorts of mistake were made—wrong assumptions about cost, equipment, climate, site and customers.

More and more, the clarion call is for a holistic approach to technology, one that takes into consideration *all* the factors of an economy, a society, politics, attitudes and skills before the fateful declaration of eureka. As Tony Killick put it in his lengthy study of the Ghanaian economy,

> [the technology] 'that will result in the highest efficiency, the greatest net benefit to the balance of payments, and the greatest spill-over effects into the rest of the economy [is that] which employs local materials and factors of production. This type of technology is, on the whole, unlikely to incorporate the most recent advances in scientific knowledge, and is therefore liable to be thought of as "inferior". It is also unlikely to be a technology which may be applied without adaptation to local conditions. Much of what went wrong with industry and agriculture was a result of inappropriate technology choices, resulting in farming fiascos and in the creation of inefficient industrial enclaves.'[1]

Recognition of the need for a holistic approach is perhaps clearest in the field of appropriate technology, because there is much to be gained if the message is heard and accepted, and more to be lost if it is not. The cry is so loud and so clear, because despite the libraries full of handbooks and plans, case studies and technical drawings, despite the theoretical, practical and moral weight behind the appropriate technology movement, the shelf which holds the reports on widespread application of the same ideas, is so far from sagging under the burden that it almost needs an anchor to keep it from floating away. The failed grain storage silos and other 'good ideas' that did not quite work stand as testimony to our shortcomings.

In TCC's experience, an 'appropriate' technology is one that optimizes the combination of available capital, raw material, skills and labour, in the most economic fashion possible, and within the social and economic goals of the nation. Ideally, the technology will follow closely on one that is already known, and will result in the creation or manufacture of a developmentally useful product at a low capital investment per unit of output. Job creation is not high on the TCC list of criteria, but inevitably there will be a considerable multiplier effect in the equation if a useful product is being manufactured. Regardless of the observance of these things in fact, all are generally understood and accepted by most organizations involved in appropriate technology. But even where they are assiduously applied, they do not always result in success. In addition to defining and choosing appropriate technologies, TCC learned something else after its first three or four years: the *transfer* of technology is as important as making the right choice, *and the one does not always follow from the other*.

The transfer of technology

The key difference between TCC and many other AT institutions was the role it began to assume, after the mid 1970s, as an implementing agency. The move to complement, or even to subordinate research and development to programming—from research and development (R & D) to the transfer of technology—is significant. It had originally been taken for granted that AT institutions should concentrate on R & D and that dissemination should be carried out by others. Much analysis of the failure to transfer appropriate technology, however, points to the fact that some research institutions are, in varying degrees, intellectually, practically or socially isolated from their intended beneficiaries and from the world in which they function; that they are inadequately linked to the support structures essential to the transfer of technology. Too often the excuse given for failure is that government, aid agencies, the private sector or some other third party did not take up a perfectly good idea and put it into action.

Had this fatal dichotomy between developer and implementer been observed by Ford, Bell, Edison and many other lesser-known 'technologists', transportation, communications and electronics would never have developed as they did. The dilemma, however, is a bit like tying a shoe-lace: most people have no difficulty in co-ordinating their left and right hands in the business of tying a competent knot. But if two individuals were asked to contribute one hand each to the tying of the same shoe-lace, the result would undoubtedly be a mess.

187

Several hands would be even more chaotic. The obvious answer, if shoe-laces are to be tied properly, is that the right hand must know what the left is doing; AT institutions must be closely co-ordinated with the bodies responsible for actually programming what they develop.

For example, a technology may have all the textbook attributes to make it 'appropriate', but if credit is not available to the intended beneficiary, it may never succeed. Many of TCC's early customers, especially those in Suame Magazine, faced this problem. Raw materials may be 'available', but getting them is sometimes another matter. Working capital, economies of scale, import licences, foreign exchange may all hinder the obvious potential for a technology as simple, say, as soapmaking. Marketing is another problem. There may be a demand for spring centre bolts, and Archibald Boateng—having worked in the TCC workshop for years—may have the expertise to make them well. But a good lathe operator is not necessarily a good salesman. Only training and experience will give him what he needs to get a quality product out into the market-place. In short, the work of an AT institution must dovetail with the work of other institutions of government and the private sector if its products are going to be put to use—with credit institutions, with those offering technical and managerial training, extension services, marketing institutions and so on. While these backward and forward linkages are absolutely essential to success, however, getting the mix just right has proven difficult, and in many cases, impossible.

Where TCC differed from other AT institutions, unintentionally at first, was that it took upon itself many of the roles that might have been left to other bodies. In the absence of appropriate linkages, and in the vacuum created by the economic decline, it became clear that 'co-ordination' would in most cases have meant failure. Training could not, therefore, be left to happenstance; knowing the elements of operating a lathe did not automatically signify competence in nut and bolt production. And while one machinist might learn the technique in a month, another might require a year. TCC provided on-the-job training—not in all cases, but where it was necessary—and sometimes over years. TCC either obtained or made much

188

of the equipment necessary for the manufacture of its products—soap-boiling tanks, caustic soda plants, palm-oil presses, lathes, milling machines. While TCC was not a credit institution, it did offer some equipment on time payments, and often assisted potential clients with cash flow projections, loan applications and credit references. Later, after an enterprise had been started, technical and management assistance was part of the TCC follow-up programme, and many clients took their first orders from TCC until they had begun to establish their own credibility with customers. TCC helped with bulk orders of raw material and tooling, and obtained import licences on behalf of groups of smaller clients who could not have done so on their own.

Client selection   Much of TCC's success can therefore be attributed to the fact that it was not only a research and development agency. It became, in effect, the body that created or co-ordinated the backward and forward linkages essential to the adoption of a new product or process. Part of its success in this area derives from an even earlier lesson learned in its first years: care in the selection of clients. Whatever the nature of the group or individual that will eventually accept and use a new technology, certain attributes must be present. There must be a basic interest in the idea and enough economic, social and political power to convert the interest into concrete action. And besides access to the technology, there must be adequate knowledge and experience to use it effectively. These factors may exist in an individual, a co-operative or a corporate body, but if they are absent, the chances of success are significantly reduced. Learning about the client became, therefore, one of the most important links in the transfer of technology, and prospective clients—groups and individuals alike—were sent forth on lengthy obstacle courses that would test their mettle and separate those with the required attributes from those without.

This lesson was not picked out of a textbook; it was learned the hard way. The brass-casters of Kurofofurom did not have the same interest in product diversification as did the village

189

Chief, and so TCC's efforts to develop alternatives to traditional castings eventually fell on stony ground. S.K. Baffoe had most of the attributes necessary to make Spider Glue a success, but he lacked the political power—in the short run—to avoid the machinations of potential competitors once he had demonstrated the success of his product. The weavers did not have it within their economic power to ensure a constant supply of cotton yarn—no one did, and so the weaving project came to a halt. Joseph Kwaako, however, had it all. He had the interest in making steel nuts and bolts. He knew the market, he had the wherewithal to get a shop built and to have the electricity supply connected. He paid for some of his first machine tools from TCC over time, but thereafter earned the creditworthiness to obtain his own capital. He had *access* to the TCC technology, but more importantly, he developed *the knowledge and ability to use it*. The same was true of most of TCC's clients in the light engineering field after about 1978, because of the care it took in client selection, development, training and follow-up, all essential parts of the transfer of technology.

Profit   TCC learned early that the profit motive was crucial to the transfer of technology in Ghana. The risks associated with productive enterprise, as opposed to the benefits that accrued from trading—especially in imported and restricted goods, had to be offset by a reasonable return on investment. Some of TCC's institutional clients—co-operatives, development agencies, government departments, the National Service Secretariat, northern mission stations, the National Council on Women and Development and others—had the interest and the ability to take and use a product or a technique effectively. Where this happened, the burden on TCC for follow-up and other development work was reduced. The intermediary institution, especially in village-based activities such as food processing, soapmaking or beekeeping, reached a large clientele that was in most cases beyond TCC's own direct grasp.

But even 'non-exploitative' development groups understood that new ideas had to be economically viable and that their

190

success was usually dependent, at least in part, on the extent of the contribution made to a project by the intended beneficiaries. The result of the beneficiaries' investment in capital and labour—whether it was called 'income generation' or 'profit'; in cash or in kind—was ultimately what determined whether or not they continued with the project. The terminology would perhaps be little more than an exercise in semantics, except that mistrust of the 'profit' motive has led to an avoidance of the small-scale private sector by development organizations and has robbed them of valuable experience, which TCC would argue is essential to an appreciation of the market-place in which true productivity is assessed and traded.

In the final analysis, few of TCC's private clients are what one would call exploitative; all have taken considerable risks, all have paid for what they received at market prices. And although profitability may have been their incentive, many have been successful because profits have been reinvested in their businesses. They have, in fact, not only demonstrated all the advantages of small-scale enterprise as listed in most studies of the subject—low capital cost, high value added, good return on investment, job creation—they have also demonstrated initiative, tenacity, and an exciting creativity that is vital to long-term development.

Product reliability and adaptation   TCC learned that if an idea was going to be successfully taken up, it had to be proven and it had to be reliable, both in itself and in the technique of manufacture. A clumsy, unreliable solar water heater, for which there was little demand, failed. Good quality, inexpensive wheel bolts were another matter entirely. The campus production units were important in this, because products which advanced beyond the idea stage still had to prove themselves under production conditions and later in the market-place where they were sold. Had TCC not run into its own problems in obtaining caustic soda, it might have taken years, if not more, to realize that the caustic soda plant was an essential part of the soapmaker's package. Without the experience of actually buying scrap on a regular basis for its

191

own manufacture of nuts and bolts, the various cost and time-saving techniques that the production unit was virtually forced to adopt would never have been developed, and the whole technology would undoubtedly be buried today, long forgotten in old filing cabinets—another good idea that for some unspecified reason had failed. The development of a cheap, simple iron foundry grew out of the Suame ITTU's direct experience of both the shortcomings and the shortages of scrap steel as a raw material.

The same product development, testing, adaptation and production approach is now regularly applied to new projects. Minimum tillage farming, for example, is still in its infancy, and until it has proven itself to farmers, it is unlikely to be adopted on a wide scale. So apart from a demonstration farm where people are trained and new techniques and crops are tested, TCC has organized a planting and spraying service in order to demystify the technique and to make some of the inputs available at reasonable cost to those who have been trained and express a further interest.

Light engineering   That TCC concentrated on light engineering was probably more a product of chance than anything else, but this, too, was a key factor in the Centre's success. It happened that those with the earliest interest in appropriate technology in Kumasi were mostly engineers at UST, members of the informal Kumasi Technology Group or the Suame Product Development Group. Their first interests were in projects which ultimately required the establishment of a machine shop and the employment of machine tool operators. It was TCC's interest in finding clients to take on early industrial products that eventually led to the development of its rationale for selling used machine tools. It was in working with the small-scale machine shops that the importance of client development came to the fore, along with the need for the Centre to provide ancillary services in the areas of credit, training, supplies, extension, follow-up and marketing. And it was in working with them that another idea, early in its conceptualization but slow in its realization, developed. TCC

192

Nuts and bolts manufactured by the TCC process; right – steel rod from which they are produced.

had to move to the clients if it was ever to shed its ivory tower image and mentality. The concept of the Intermediate Technology Transfer Units was critical to this, and probably accounted as much as anything else for the credibility the Centre today enjoys in Kumasi's informal sector.

The importance of light engineering to the work of TCC was significant, because much of the Centre's ability to take on other activities sprang directly from it. The dozen engineering workshops established in Suame Magazine by TCC contained 65 machine tools, roughly ten times the number that had existed in the entire Magazine ten years earlier. These shops had developed a capacity that ranged from the manufacture of good quality industrial components—nuts and bolts, piston rings, sprockets, gears—to finished machines. But they were also directly linked to TCC's rural industrial development programme in that much of the equipment developed and once produced in TCC's own workshop, was now being produced by clients in Suame. The palm-oil press was, by the mid-1980s, being made exclusively by TCC clients, as were most soap-boiling tanks. From TCC and its engineering clients came products that benefited agriculture, rural industry, food processing and woodworking. Minimum tillage farming required the TCC maize planter, developed at the ITTU. Half a dozen food processing machines were in production. The circular sawbenches and wood-turning lathes started the use of cheap off-cuts from big sawmills, and pointed the woodworking industry into new areas of manufacture. TCC introduced new products for the woodworking industry as well: the wooden broadloom, the Kenya top-bar beehive, soap-cutting tables, moulding and packing boxes, and even crates for the breweries.

Once the overall approach had been developed and small workshops like SIS Engineering and Josbarko began to emerge as viable, going concerns, new products such as corn mills, spark plug extenders and Volkswagen engine bushings could be developed without great reliance on TCC. By the early 1980s, some of the clients had essentially taken over the role that TCC played in its early years, *becoming small appropriate technology centres themselves*, developing products, testing their practicality and economic viability in the market-place, and then putting them into production. The importance of this development cannot be overestimated, for it makes all the difference between reliance on an external agency such as TCC and the beginnings of a society's ability to carry out its own technological development. In Ghana, it is the start of the industrial revolution that was short-circuited by the colonial era.

Continuity　　A final clue to TCC's ability to transfer technology effectively has been its great fortune in attracting many talented individuals to its endeavours. While a very small number have been recruited externally, most were attracted to TCC from other positions within Ghana, and came with solid experience behind them. Although John Powell had not been in Ghana long when he became Director, his guidance of TCC over its first fourteen years gave the Centre a continuity, a sense of direction and a memory that few development organizations anywhere enjoy. The people employed under

USAID and CIDA contracts were all recruited within Ghana rather than externally, which made them more productive than most people on technical assistance contracts. And of the senior staff, more than half stayed with TCC for five years or more, while several key players remained beyond ten.

The way ahead

If one is to judge by the uptake from its efforts and the relatively small investment made in it, both in local currency and foreign exchange, TCC probably ranks among the most successful appropriate technology institutions in the world. Hundreds of small-scale urban and rural enterprises today earn income from technologies introduced to Ghana by TCC; the job creation effect is considerable and the foreign exchange savings to the country are enormous. An array of TCC products and techniques are at work on farms, in industry and villages throughout Ghana, and some of what the Centre has learned has been passed on to half a dozen other countries. Most important of all, a capacity and a potential for further development, quite independent of TCC, has been put in place.

This book has argued the case for appropriate technology, and has discussed both the constraints it faced and the ways in which the constraints were overcome by the Technology Consultancy Centre. The problem in coming out unequivocally in favour of appropriate technology in Ghana, however, is not in finding examples of success stories, but in making a quantifiable estimate of the impact that would result from a shift in investment from large or medium-scale to small enterprise. Statistical analysis of the sectors that stand to gain or lose from such a policy change is so bad that it borders on disgraceful. This is a criticism not only of Ghana's academic community and successive governments, but of aid agencies and lending institutions. Despite the battalions of consultants that have trooped past Ghana's industrial sector over the years, despite repeated acknowledgement of the values in job creation and the economies in capital investment among small-scale rural and urban industries, the data base is so uneven that if the fault did not lie with the very institutions that could correct it, it would almost justify the wastage that has resulted from them ignoring it.

For example, a 1974 World Bank study showed that the value added per thousand cedis of capital invested in large-scale industry was 289 cedis. This compared favourably with a 1976 figure of 205 cedis, calculated by Checchi and Company.[2] The comparison for enterprises employing fewer than ten people was very different, however. The Bank said that the value added was 1,455 cedis per 1,000 invested; Checchi said it was half that. While the overall conclusion certainly favours small-scale industry, the similar figures for large-scale industry and the vast difference for small suggest that the data base of the latter is probably insufficient to justify serious consideration. One might assume that these two studies, one based on 133 enterprises and the other on only 33, would have been complemented in the ensuing decade by further studies. If they have, none have been quoted in any of the documents used to justify and describe the hundreds of millions of dollars in credits, loans or aid programmes to Ghana up to 1985. In fact, it was a 1983 Bank report on the manufacturing sector that quoted from the original 1974 study which exhorted analysts and planners to 'pay increased attention to conditions and performance in the small-scale sector', noting the 'virtual absence of data on small-scale establishments since 1973.'

Part of the difficulty in obtaining reliable data on small-scale enterprise is that it cannot be done quickly or easily. The large-scale manufacturing sector is small, relatively concentrated, and keeps records, all of which facilitate study. A thorough analysis of the thousands of workshops in Suame Magazine alone, where few records are kept and questions may be answered in a variety of ways depending upon the affiliation of the questioner and the perceptions or suspicions of the respondent, is a much more daunting task. Nor is it likely to be conducted effectively by outsiders with limited experience of the sector and of Ghana. Although such study and analysis fall outside the mandate that TCC developed for itself, it could conceivably and logically be carried out by the Centre, given adequate support from the university, government and

196

interested external agencies. Without it, however, examples of what is possible, remain only that—examples.

The first and most basic stage for an AT institution is the choice and development of appropriate technologies. This level has been well defined and generally attained on an international basis. The successful transfer of appropriate technology is more difficult, however, and although TCC reached this second stage, it did not happen quickly, or easily. If there is a lesson, it is that the spread of new technologies in a weakened, dual economy will not happen rapidly, and will not happen at all without a great deal of support. In Ghana, TCC had to build its own support infrastructure, achieving success mostly despite, rather than because of policies, attitudes and programmes of university, government and the international development community.

The third level of appropriate technology—widespread dissemination—cannot be reached without strong support from government and the international development community. Obstacles to small-scale industrial and rural development have to be removed, while strong incentives and support structures have to be created. This will entail more than simply announcing another credit scheme, or establishing another set of extension agents. It will not come about through the creation of the 'small-scale development boards' that are so common in Third World countries, unless they are given the competent, interdisciplinary staff, the budgets, the authority and the marching orders adequate to undertake the comprehensive analysis that will be the precursor to real and meaningful policy change. Such an effort is deserving of international support, not the amateurish, tokenistic, sluggardly tied-aid projects of the past, but real support which expands access to choices of technology, raw materials, technical assistance and markets.

The technology issue in the Third World can only become larger and more pronounced as time passes; multidimensional support and policy commitment at the highest level are therefore essential if Ghana, or any other country for that matter, is to break out of the downward economic spiral in which it has been trapped, if it is to turn working *examples* of

197

appropriate technology, into meaningful substitutes for the large-scale, capital-intensive, moribund investments of the past.

There is no clear or obvious route to the future, but perhaps the last word should be left to E.F. Schumacher, who did more than anyone to popularize and advance the notion of appropriate technology in this century. In his posthumously published work, *A Guide for the Perplexed*,[3] Schumacher wrote of Dante—in the *Divine Comedy*—waking up and finding himself 'in the horrible dark wood where he had never meant to go, his good intention to make the ascent up the mountain . . . of no avail; he first had to descend into the inferno.' In likening the modern world to Dante's inferno, Schumacher noted some positive recent developments. 'Some people are no longer angry when told that restoration must come from within; the belief that everything is "politics" and that radical rearrangements of "system" will suffice to save civilization is no longer held with the same fanaticism as it was held twenty five years ago.' He noted changes in attitudes, approaches to environment, consumption, food and health, experiments in what he called voluntary simplicity, in response to the fact that 'faith in modern man's omnipotence is wearing thin.'

'Can we rely on it that a "turning around" will be accomplished by enough people quickly enough to save the modern world?' he asked. 'Whatever answer is given . . . will mislead. The answer "Yes" would lead to complacency; the answer "No" to despair. It is desirable to leave these perplexities behind us and get down to work.'

References and Further Reading

All statistics, unless otherwise noted, are drawn from official govern-
ment and international sources.

Chapter 2
1. Lester Pearson, *Partners in Development* (World Bank, 1970).
2. E.F. Schumacher, *Small is Beautiful: A Study of Economics as if*
   People Mattered (Blond & Briggs, London, 1973).
3. Ibid, 143.

Chapter 3
1. Central Bureau of Statistics.
2. Sally Holterman, *Intermediate Technology in Ghana: The Experi-*
   ence of Kumasi University's Technology Consultancy Centre
   (IT Publications, London, 1979).
3. John Powell, An African Comb (1983) unpublished.
4. Ibid, ch. 14.

Chapter 4
1. *South* (July 1985).

Chapter 5
1. Nicholas Jéquier and Gerard Blanc, *The World of Appropriate*
   Technology (OECD, 1983). Taken from Marilyn Carr, Ed., *The*
   AT Reader; Theory and Practice in Appropriate Technology (IT
   Publications, London, 1985), 9.
2. B.T. Adjorlolo, *An Essay on Appropriate Technology* (SIS
   Engineering Ltd, Kumasi, 1985).
3. Checchi and Company, Small Scale Industry Development in
   Ghana Washington (1976) unpublished.
4. World Bank (1974) and Small Scale Industry Development in
   Ghana.
5. *Small is Beautiful*, 238.
6. *Small is Beautiful*, 234.
7. Stephen Salter, *New Scientist* (1982). Taken from *AT Reader*,
   65–6.
8. African Comb.

Chapter 6
1. Small Scale Industry Development in Ghana.
2. N. Florida, *et al*, Small Scale Industry in Ghana (1977) unpublished.
3. Canadian International Development Agency, Evaluation Report on the ITTU at Suame Magazine (1981) unpublished.
4. ——, End of Project/Termination Report, ITTU, Ghana (1983) unpublished.
5. Stephen Adjare, *The Golden Insect: A Handbook on Beekeeping for Beginners* (IT Publications, London, 1981).

Chapter 7
1. A. Mazrui and M. Tidy, *Nationalism and New States in Africa* (Heinemann, London, 1984), 248.
2. John Powell and J. Quansah, *Case Study No. 2; Josbarko Enterprise* (TCC, Ghana, 1981).
3. Small Scale Industry Development in Ghana.
4. 'ITTU Engineers Achieve Another Feat', *People's Daily Graphic* (Accra, 6 May 1980).
5. 'Palm Kernel Powers Steel Furnaces', *Ghanaian Times* (Accra, 6 May 1980).

Chapter 8
1. Tony Killick, *Development Economics in Action; A Study of Economic Policies in Ghana* (Heinemann, London, 1978).
2. W.F. Buchele and J.K. Campbell, *Feasibility of Using Intermediate Technology to Produce Agricultural Tools and Machinery in Ghana* (1975) unpublished.
3. Peter Donkor, 'A Hand-operated Screw Press for Extracting Palm Oil', *Appropriate Technology*, Vol. 5, No. 4 (February 1979).
4. 'Low-cost Palm Oil Press', *International Agricultural Development* (January/February 1985).
5. C.F. Garman, *Small Scale Farm Mechanization for Zero Tillage in Humid and Sub-humid Tropics* (IITA).
6. Ibid.
7. K. Ampong-Nyarko, *A Review of the Safety Aspects of Using Paraquat and Glyphosate* (Crops Research Institute of Kwadoso, Kumasi, 1981).

Chapter 9
1. *Intermediate Technology in Ghana.*

Chapter 10
1. African Comb.

2. Stephen Adjare, '150,000 Industrious Workers Burned to Death', *Ghana Bee News* (TCC, Kumasi, 1982).

Chapter 11
1. Richard Whitcombe and Marilyn Carr, *Appropriate Technology Institutions; A Review* (ITDG, London, 1982).

Chapter 12
1. *Development Economics in Action.*
2. Small Scale Industry Development in Ghana.
3. E.F. Schumacher, *A Guide for the Perplexed* (Abacus, London, 1978).

Further Reading

James Anquandah, *Discovering Ghana's Past* (Longmans, London, 1982).

B.A. Ateng and L.P. Mweithi, 'Economic Efficiency and the Mechanization of Small Farms', *Appropriate Mechanization of Small Farms in Africa* (Association for the Advancement of Agricultural Sciences in Africa).

E. Date-Bah, *Rural Women, Their Activities and Technology in Ghana; An Overview* (WEP/ILO, Geneva, 1981).

S.J. de Boer, *Small Scale Industry Development in Six West African Countries* (UNIDO, undated).

Development Alternatives Inc., *Improved Rural Technology in Africa* (USAID, Washington, 1977).

Peter Donkor, *Case Study No. 3; Soap Pilot Plant* (TCC, Ghana, 1981).

——, Small Scale Soapmaking for Developing Countries (1975) unpublished.

Cameron Duodu, 'Twixt the Devil and the TUC', *South* (July 1985).

Economist Intelligence Unit, *Quarterly Economic Review of Ghana, Sierra Leone and Liberia,* No. 2 (1985).

John B. Free, *Bees and Mankind* (George Allen & Unwin, London, 1982).

G.K. Helleiner, *International Economic Disorder: Essays in North/South Relations* (MacMillan, London, 1980).

F.W. Lukey, *The Ashanti Economy Towards the Year 2000* (TCC, Ghana, 1980).

——, *Case Study No. 1: Lab. Products Ltd* (TCC, Part 1, 1978; Part 2, 1980).

——, *Evaluation Report on the Intermediate Technology Transfer Unit at Suame Magazine* (CIDA, 1981).

——, *Minimum Tillage Farming* (TCC, Ghana, 1982).

——, *Some Areas of Business Opportunity in Ashanti over the Next Twenty Years* (TCC, Ghana, 1980).

——, 'Steel Bolts: A Hand Forging Process', *Appropriate Technology*, Vol. 4, No. 1 (May 1977).

R. Mitchell, Ghana: Small Scale Enterprise Development (1985) unpublished.

F. Oduro-Boateng, Method for Production of Fingerlings at Lake Bosomtwi Basin (1984) unpublished.

V. Pakenham, *The Noonday Sun* (Methuen, London, 1985).

John Powell, *An Intermediate Technology Role for a University in the Third World* (TCC, Ghana, 1977).

——, *Inputs of the Science Departments of the Universities in Relation to the Economic Recovery Programme* (TCC, Ghana, 1985).

——, *Appropriate Technology in India* (TCC, Ghana, 1978).

——, *Background Paper on Development of Endogenous Technologies* (TCC, Ghana, 1982).

——, 'Machine Tools in Informal Industries in Africa: An Appropriate Technology for Thread Cutting', *Appropriate Technology*, Vol. 8, No. 2 (September 1981).

——, Other People's Profits (1985) unpublished.

——, *Report of DAPIT Project Activities, 1984* (TCC, Ghana, 1985).

——, Report of Director's Visit to Tamale ITTU (December 1984 and March 1985).

——, The Selection of Appropriate Technology for the Ghanaian Entrepreneur (TCC, Ghana, 1978).

——, *The Transfer of Appropriate Technology as a Strategy in Rural Development* (TCC, Ghana, undated).

——, 'University Involvement in Appropriate Technology', *Appropriate Technology*, Vol. 6, No. 4 (February 1980).

——, University Involvement in Appropriate Technology: Report of a Visit to the University of Technology at Lae, PNG.

——, and E.O. Asare, *Appropriate Technology for Small Farms: The Ghana Experience* (TCC, Ghana, 1984).

E.F. Schumacher, *Good Work* (Jonathan Cape, London, 1979).

Technology Consultancy Centre, Kumasi, *Annual Reviews*, Nos. 1–12; 1972–84 (TCC, Ghana).

——, *Balance Sheet and Accounts*, 1981, 1982, 1983 (TCC, Ghana).

——, *A Brief History of TCC Beekeeping Activity in Ghana* (TCC, Ghana, undated).

——, *Ghana Bee News*, quarterly journal, 1981 through 1985 (TCC, Ghana).
N. Terdre, 'Ghana's Big Cocoa Shake-up', *South* (May 1985).
S.A. Whyte, 'Distribution, Trophic Relationships and Breeding Habits of the Fish Populations in a Tropical Lake Basin', *Journal of Zoology* (London, 1975).
Kwasi Wiafe-Annor, *Bosomtwe, The Sacred Lake* (Wavelight Publications, Accra, 1979).